Illustrated

PIPER

BUYER'S ★ GUIDE™

Tom Murphy and Hans Halberstadt

Motorbooks International
Publishers & Wholesalers ®

First published in 1993 by Motorbooks International Publishers & Wholesalers, PO Box 2, 729 Prospect Avenue, Osceola, WI 54020 USA

Motorbooks International books are also available at discounts in bulk quantity for industrial or sales-promotional use. For details write to Special Sales Manager at the Publisher's address

Library of Congress Cataloging-in-Publication Data
    Murphy, Tom.
    Illustrated Piper buyer's guide/Tom Murphy, Hans halberstadt.
        p. cm. —(Motorbooks International illustrated buyer's guide series)
    Includes index.
    ISBN 0-87938-786-6
    1. Piper airplanes—Purchasing. I. Halberstadt, Hans.
        II. Title. III. Series.
    TL686.P5M87   1993
    629.133'343—dc20   93-43190

On the front cover: A Piper Cruiser.

On the back cover: Top, a 1981 Saratoga SP. Bottom, an Aerostar 601. *Piper*

Printed and bound in the United States of America

Contents

Preface

If you and I are talking to each other through the medium of this book, you are probably as interested in airplanes as I am. Piper airplanes to be specific. Perhaps you are just beginning your adventure in the air as a student pilot and think that you would like to own the airplane that teaches you to fly. Maybe you already hold a pilot's license, have been renting aircraft for a while with the intention to buy your own airplane one day. Or, you are flying your own plane now, but would like to see what's available in the Piper line. Whatever your reason for reading this book, I sincerely hope that you and I have a good time and I can share some knowledge about Mr. Piper and his airplanes from Lock Haven, Pennsylvania.

We'll get to know a little about the man behind the airplane, but most of our time will be spent studying the airplanes themselves. This book is intended to help anyone, be they pilots or not, to learn what Pipers are all about, what they can do, what you can do with them and what you can reasonably expect out of a particular model in the way of performance.

Before we get too deep into the meat of the book, a word of caution is in order. This book in no way replaces the pilot's operating handbook (POH) for your airplane. The airplane flight manual approved by the Federal Aviation Administration (FAA) is the official source of operating parameters and performance information. This information assumes you have an airplane with a certain amount of factory and optional equipment, flown under standard conditions, and should not be considered applicable for all situations. In planning each flight, we urge the pilot to allow for a comfortable performance reserve. At all times, the POH is the final authority on operation and specifications for your aircraft. Consult it before every flight. I go back to the POH for an airplane that I owned a few years ago and I'm constantly amazed at how much detail has slipped my mind. Say I've been flying a Saratoga SP for the last eleven months and a friend of mine wants me to check out a Cherokee 235 that he's considering buying. Now you would think that after flying a 300hp, turbocharged, retractable, six-seat single for 230hr, getting into a 235hp, fixed gear four-seater and taking it for a test ride would be no problem—just preflight and go. Well, I did that once and proved to myself and the man trying to sell the airplane that I really knew how to make a fool out of myself. Didn't make any big-time mistakes or I wouldn't be staring at my Macintosh while writing this book. What I did do was to forget little things like takeoff speed, pattern speed, and stall speed, all the insignificant, unimportant things. Sure flew behind the airplane that day!

Since then, any airplane that I haven't been in within the last 90 days gets its POH read at least once before I go turn gas into noise, and I advise that you do the same. Always fly safely. Plan your flights on the ground when you have the luxury of being able to look at a checklist or chart without having to worry about the scenery moving past at high speed. There's always time to plan before you turn the prop, no matter how badly you want to get home or how fast the daylight is fading. As I have learned the hard way, no one needs to fly *right now*. Other arrangements can always be made and passengers don't make the decisions—you do.

This brings to mind having 7gal of fuel left in the tanks of an airplane that burns 35gph; being 20 miles from the airport and thinking about the fuel stop I passed up because I was in a hurry to get back home. The Good Fairy was kind enough to put a landing strip just off my right wing slightly before I was going to look for a long patch of highway. The Practical Joke Department ensured that it was a restricted military base, not open to anyone. And the Surprise Party Department let me be met by two gentlemen in uniform, replete with M-16s. But that's another story for another time. I've done a few dumb things in aviation and a couple of smart ones. Perhaps if a book like this one had been available before I started buying airplanes, I wouldn't have made the mistakes that I did. But then I wouldn't be able to tell you some of the stories in this book, would I?

I would like to thank both Doug and Steve Remington, owners of The Flying Country Club, an FBO at Reid-Hillview Airport in San Jose, for supplying me with enough material and help to write this book. Also, much thanks to Piper for their airplanes and pictures. May they prosper for many years to come.

Introduction

My first experience with owning a Piper came in 1978 with the purchase of a white and blue 1967 Cherokee 140 with only 1,245hr total time airframe and engine (TTAF&E). I purchased it from a 72-year-old man who had bought it as a new airplane in late 1968. He said that he was getting a little shaky on the controls and didn't fly it more than three or four hours per month so he thought he would just rent airplanes for the next ten years or so. The price was right and I wanted an airplane worse than Custer wanted faster horses, so money changed hands. The whole transaction was handled by a fixed base operator (FBO) at Reid-Hillview Airport, five miles south of San Jose International. I had been renting Piper Archers and Warriors for the past two years before I decided to bite the bullet and own my own airplane: I knew I was an expert on airplanes, therefore buying one would be no sweat. I could hand over money and simply fly away. Dumb, dumb, dumb. I know everyone has to start somewhere, so I thought I'd start stupid. Worked, too!

There I was with just enough knowledge to be real dangerous, enough pilot's ego to be obnoxious, and $10,000 cash, ready to walk into trouble. I was very fortunate in that the Cherokee was being listed through a reputable FBO, whose owner took one look at me and either took pity or couldn't believe that I was *really* that stupid. He took the time to teach a young man all about the ins and outs of aircraft ownership. And I've continued to learn all these years. It has been said before:

You don't start to learn about airplanes until your name is on the registration—very true.

What should you be looking for in general when contemplating an aircraft purchase? How does buying an aircraft differ from other types of purchases?

The first item to be addressed is the amount of money available. Not just for the cost of the airplane, but also for the cost of the entire transaction. From the initial avgas used to fly a demonstration flight to the cost of a pre-purchase inspection, the expenses will mount. If the airplane checks out ok and the deal looks like it will go through, then a title search must be made to ensure that the airplane is free of any liens. An insurance company must be contacted to arrange coverage. A decision must be made about who will cover the cost of any necessary repairs found during the pre-purchase. Will the owner pay for the repairs and the buyer take care of the inspection? Will any needed repairs have to be completed before the title changes hands?

With a working idea of the costs involved, now it's time to look for an airplane. Most prospective buyers have a general idea of what they want. The first-time shopper might not know whether he wants a Piper or some other brand of aircraft, but he does know that he's been flying a Piper Archer and wants a similar single-engine airplane in the 180hp bracket. A pilot with 300-400hr in the logbook, all of it flying singles, might want to move up to a multi-engine plane, such as a Seneca.

Some places to look are: *Trade-A-Plane,* the yellow paper published three times a month in Tennessee (PO Box 509, 410 West 4th Street, Crossville, TN 38557). This paper covers the entire US and some foreign countries. *Pacific Flyer* on the West Coast, or its sister publication *Atlantic Flyer,* in the east (both reached through 3355 Mission Ave., Suite 213, Oceanside, CA 92054), will have aircraft and parts for sale. The last two are fun to read, even though they're a little on the weird side at times. They enjoy flying and sarcasm, not necessarily in that order. All the above are available at most airport gift shops, or you can send money and they will send you a subscription.

Whatever airplane is selected, the basic steps prior to purchase are the same. Initially, an airplane must be located that fits the requirements as far as type and price. Then the owner and prospective buyer usually go for a demo flight of an hour or so. During the demo, the buyer has a chance to see how this particular airplane differs from what he has been flying in the past. He gets to sample the characteristics unique to this airplane, how it feels, where the controls are, how it reacts to simple maneuvers. This is definitely not the time to try to show the owner any latent aerobatic talents.

Once back on the ground, if the prospective buyer is happy with what he has just flown, then the next step, the pre-purchase inspection, must be done. The best way to handle this is to pick a shop that hasn't done business with the owner in the past. If you are at a small airport with limited operations, the possibility of moving the airplane to a different airport, with better facilities, must be considered. Most of the time, if a deposit is made with the owner, some type of agreement can be reached, and the airplane can be ferried to another airport.

Now is the time to contact your insurance company with pertinent information on the airplane. Ask the owner if the airplane will be covered through his insurance while it's moved for the inspection, and afterwards while arrangements are made for the payoff. If he replies to the negative, then it would be wise to have your coverage in force before the airplane departs its home airport.

If time permits, check with the manager of the shop doing the inspection to see if he minds having the buyer work with the mechanic doing the work. Three or four hours spent with the mechanic going over the airplane will be more informative than two days with the aircraft manual.

The first items checked are the logbooks. Murphy's Law #1: No logbooks, no sale—unless you want to take on a project of unknown proportions.

Initially, the mechanic checks the logs to see if all the Airworthiness Directives (ADs) have been done. ADs are repairs that must be performed on the airplane, sometimes before it can fly again. Any not shown as done will have to be taken care of before the airplane can be signed off as safe to fly again.

For instance, in 1970 an AD was issued that covered replacing the factory bolts in the landing gear of various Cherokee 140s. These bolts were of the wrong strength, and had the nasty habit of breaking off on landing. That's one AD to make sure was done.

After checking all the ADs, the mechanic will then read the rest of the logbook to see what type of life the airplane has enjoyed. With the general aviation fleet nearing a 25-year average, the chances are good that something, other than oil changes and inspections, has happened to the airplane in the past.

Then it's time to take off covers and inspection plates for a look at the insides. After everything is gone over, which usually takes 4hr, the mechanic has a good idea of the condition of the airplane. He will also have a checklist of what needs to be repaired. Rest assured, he will find problem areas needing work. Some items will have to be done right away; some can be left until later.

Normally the way this is handled, is that the seller will pay for any major repairs and the buyer pays for the inspection. However, this is subject to how well the buyer bargains and how badly the seller wants to part with his airplane.

As mentioned above, along with an inspection, a title search must be done before parting with any money. The title has to be clear of any liens and not held as security in a loan.

At this time, it might be prudent to join The Aircraft Owners and Pilots Association (AOPA), 421 Aviation Way, Frederick, MD 21701. They have a multitude of services, from title search (800-654-4700) to insurance and financial advice. Once in the AOPA, be prepared to find copious quantities of aviation literature arriving in the mailbox from them and various aviation supply companies.

The AOPA and Airman Records department in Oklahoma City have a standard package that includes a rush title search, a search of all ADs, and a search of any accident involving any particular airplane. This runs $115 and they will take plastic. A basic title search runs $35, with an additional $5 for a rush job, all of which can be handled over the phone with a minimum of fuss.

Now it's time for money to change hands. Most aircraft purchases are financed, usually through a lending institution familiar with airplanes, as an average bank isn't knowledgeable about aircraft values, so tends to stay away from aviation loans. See if it's possible to get pre-qualified for financing prior to looking for an airplane.

Most lenders will authorize a set amount of money based on previous credit history. Find out how their lending policy operates. Will they lend 80 percent of wholesale, 90 percent of purchase price, or what? Knowing the financial limits in advance will make locating an airplane much easier.

Then it's time to fill out a bill of sale and registration (both forms available at any airport gift shop, or through AOPA), hand over the agreed upon price, and become the owner of the airplane.

Once you have your own plane, things like oil pressure, cylinder temperature, and radio condition become much more important. Flying the same plane on a regular basis will teach you all its quirks—every plane is different. You'll soon fly it enough that you will recognize any small change in operation. After a while, any abnormal noise or vibration will become very apparent, any rough running will grab your attention immediately. (Yes, I know that all airplanes are guaranteed to go into "automatic rough" when crossing mountains or open water—this has nothing to do with your nerves or paranoia.)

Now that you have spent some time learning about how to buy an airplane, it's time to figure out what all the airplanes are, how they differ from each other, and what all the numbers and strange abbreviations mean. You knew that Piper built Archers and Warriors, you have seen a Malibu parked in the hangar across from the flight line, and you've seen a lot of twin-engine airplanes around with Piper's name on them. What are all these airplanes and what do they do?

That's what this book is all about—Piper aircraft. Early models from the first J-3 Cub to the latest and biggest Cheyenne 400 LS will be covered in detail. What they are, how much they will carry, how fast, how far, all the specifications are in this book. The good points will be covered, the not so good also. Some of my adventures will be told, usually as educational tools.

Now that the entire fleet is aging past twenty years, with a lot of hours on the average plane, condition and care is more important than age of airframe. Better a 1976 Archer with 2,104hr total time on the airframe (TTAF) and a factory remanufactured (REMAN) engine than a 1986 with 5,300 TTAF and 1,700hr since major overhaul (SMOH). While we're on the subject of hours and engines, one point comes to mind that you want to consider when looking at something with wings and a rebuilt engine.

There are many levels of engine reconditioning out there in airplaneland and each one is different from the other. First you will see an airplane advertised with a "rebuilt" engine. What this covers is anything from me tearing down an engine in my garage and doing a basic ring, bearing, and gasket overhaul using all the original parts that still fall within the manufacturers specs, to buying parts through a mail-order house and putting in "well, it's almost legal" components, to a complete replacement of everything that moves by an engine shop with a run-up on the test stand included.

Next on the list is the "overhaul to factory specs." This means that some parts have seen each other before, but the whole engine is put together to the specifications on the blueprints of the company that first built the engine. All parts fall within the factory's parameters for tolerance. This should be a better go-through, with more new parts, than a basic rebuild. As an aside, I once watched a man pull his Cessna's engine apart three times in as many months while he was trying to figure out why it didn't run as well as it did before he disassembled it for a rebuild. You want to be the next owner of that airplane? Me neither.

Next we come to REMAN engines. This means that the engine has been assembled to factory new specifications: everything that goes into the engine will be either new or with no wear. Usually all the internal parts except the crank and rods are new. The engine cases are reused only if they fall within factory tolerances for new parts. If any part doesn't meet the specs, it's not in the engine, even if the part is good enough to go in a rebuilt or overhauled engine. And, given human nature and the price of aircraft parts, it probably will find its way between a set of cases. The latest airplane that I have flown was just treated to a REMAN engine. It's a Piper Saratoga SP (see chapter 5), with a 300hp turbocharged Lycoming TIO-540 up front, tied to a constant speed prop. The owner told me that at last glance, the REMAN, complete with prop rebuild and new accessories, had set him back $45,000 (here everybody gasps), with a few small items still to be worked out. Ah, yes . . . $40,000 for an engine and it wasn't even a new one. Not that you would expect to see that kind of money on the front of your Warrior, but it does give one room to ponder.

When you overhaul an engine today, the cost of pulling it off the airplane, tearing it down, and filling it with all those expensive parts is so high that unless you are on your fifth year as an aviation-engine rebuilder, it only makes sense to go for the best when overhaul time comes around. Installing a REMAN engine usually can be done on an exchange basis, so downtime is kept to a minimum—an important consideration if the airplane is paying for itself as a lease-back. It doesn't make any money in the hangar.

I have yet to mention the option of replacing a runout engine with one that is factory new. Unless there is a reason to go with brand new, such as a swap to a larger cubic inch or higher horsepower engine, going the new route can be very expensive. As the scope of this book is to deal with used airplanes, I think that going with a REMAN makes more sense than paying 40–50 percent more for a factory new product.

If you are contemplating buying an airplane with a powerplant less than three years old, ask to see the receipts for the work done. The engine logbook will have the date of overhaul and the type of exchange or rebuild, but a handful of paperwork will tell you who did it and what new parts were installed at the time it was apart. Also, something else to look at is the number of times that the engine cases have been reused. If they are on the first go-round with a rebuild, then you're probably not going to have any strange problems—as in a hard-to-find oil leak or the dreaded cracked case—pop up after the first few hundred hours of running time. Cases, like any other part, have a useful life measured in hours. The first or second rebuild is usually ok, the third time around I'd be real leery. As said above, saving a few bucks at overhaul time isn't worth having a windshield turn black with oil as you take off. Don't try to cut corners with the parts that make an airplane fly. You don't want to be the first person at the scene of an accident.

We expect an airplane engine to put up with much ham-handed operation during its run to TBO. Poor mixture leaning at altitude or its opposite, forgetting to enrich the mixture on descent, causing the engine to run very lean, are the two most common faults. Shock cooling an engine by pulling back the power to idle and diving for the ground when you find yourself high, hot, and too close to the landing field, can cause the cylinders to crack from a rapid thermal drop. Running at full power on a very hot day, causing all the temperature gauges to run close to, or even in the red, will have a detrimental effect on engine life.

People sometimes compare an airplane engine to an automobile engine in terms of useful life. After all, most any new car engine will cheerfully operate for well over 125,000 miles if it has its oil changed when we remember, or every 20,000 miles, whichever comes last. Also, tuneups these days don't amount to much more than changing spark plugs every 30,000 miles and replacing anything that breaks during the life span of the car. If a car motor requires so little maintenance, why does an airplane engine need so much more to run just 2,000hr?

What most people don't take into consideration is that a car engine spends most of its life putting out about 10–15 percent of rated power, of while an airplane engine runs at a much higher power loading all of its life. A 360ci Lycoming will put out 180hp at 2,700rpm while a motor like the 3,000cc (183ci) V-6 in a Dodge Stealth will produce 300hp at 5,800rpm, 120 more horses out of a 117ci smaller engine. However, if the Stealth engine had to run at 75 percent power (225hp) all the time it operated, for 1–4hr at a time, it would wear out long before it reached 2,000hr of operation. Considering that 225hp will propel the Stealth way in excess of 100mph, this comparison becomes mostly philosophical as barring the Silver State 100 Race in Nevada, there aren't too many places where you could run the Dodge for an hour at 75 percent power without getting to play Perry Mason before a real live judge.

A few years ago, I purchased a 1960 Beechcraft Debonair from a private party. The airplane was in the middle of an annual inspection, so I took the opportunity to go work on the airplane with the mechanic doing the inspection. The idea wasn't so much to save money as to get to know my new purchase. He was fairly meticulous about opening up the airplane and making sure that all was as Mr. Beech had intended. I changed brakes. I changed wheel bearings. I stop-drilled and riveted every crack I found, down to a two-inch split in the engine heat shield. I even fabricated new sheet-metal covers for the wing-to-fuselage bolts. We jacked it way up off the ground so the gear could be swung and gear door fit readjusted. I worked for three weeks on this airplane before I ever got to fly it.

One day, as we were checking the tachometer against true prop speed with a strobe, I asked the mechanic about checking the fuel-injection system for proper calibration. He informed me that it was all right, as he had recently done some work on it and it was good at that time. Well, after his being so nit-picking about the rest of the airplane, I figured he was right about the fuel injection.

Anybody want to guess the rest of the story—what happened on my first flight? Yup, less than one hour into the flight from San Jose to Reno, I was cleared to begin my descent into the airport. As I pulled the power back to begin losing altitude from 13,500ft over the Sierra Nevadas, the engine began to run rough and miss badly. I played with the mixture and power settings only to be rewarded with the sound of silence. The loudest noise that could be heard was the pounding of my heart and the rush of wind past the cockpit. I figured that the best thing to do was to make sure I could get to the airport first, then tell the tower of my predicament second. I feathered the prop to extend the glide range and it slowly came to a stop. My wife turned to me with great big eyes and asked me why I shut the engine off, were we in trouble? Well, as I was more than a little occupied at the time, about all I could manage to tell her was, "Something broke, honey. Don't worry though, we'll make it just fine." My cardinal rule about crossing mountains always was to have at least 2,000ft between the bottom of the airplane and the tops of the mountains; this time I was real happy to have followed my rules. I was over Mt. Rose, 10,776ft MSL, heading for Reno-Cannon Airport, 4,412 MSL and 12nm away. After the airplane was stabilized in an 800fpm descent, I called Reno to advise them of my problem. I was fairly sure that we would have no problem making the airport as by that time we still had 4,500ft to lose before we were at pattern altitude.

Reno asked if I wanted to declare an emergency. I couldn't see how declaring would help the airplane fly any farther, so I declined.

Reno cleared us for landing—any runway. They asked if I thought I could make Runway 25 so as not to block the incoming jet traffic on Runway 16R. We had arrived over the airport by that time, 2,000ft above the 5,212ft MSL pattern altitude. I saw that too much altitude was going to be a problem, so I told Reno Tower I'd extend a bit and enter Runway 25's pattern on a left downwind.

Then I figured I didn't want to be on a long downwind and run out of airspeed, altitude, and ideas all at the same time; better keep it in tight and, if needed, slip to a landing.

We managed to put it on the ground without further drama. The airplane had stopped just short of the intersection of Runways 25 and 16R. It took 20min to get towed off the active over to Reno Jet Center, where we were to learn that the fuel-injection unit was worn so badly, a new one was needed.

One week later, I flew back to Reno on a commercial flight. The mechanic who worked on the airplane and I had a nice 30min flight around the airport, shooting touch-and-gos while checking out the new fuel-injection metering unit. After that, the trip home was quite uneventful.

The point being, if you are going to overhaul your engine, don't scrimp on the important items. You don't have to spend all of next year's income rebuilding—just make sure the parts are right.

Joining a type club is a very good way to learn more about your particular airplane. Almost every aircraft flying has some group of followers who have already experienced all the problems and repairs particular to your aircraft. The Cherokee Pilot's Association, PO Box 7927, Tampa, FL 33673, or The Cub Club, PO Box 2002, Mt. Pleasant, MI 48804, are two organizations that deal with the single-engine Pipers. The International Comanche Society, PO Box 400, Grant, NE 69140, is dedicated to the care and feeding of Piper Comanches, from the 180hp version to the hot-rod of the fleet, the Comanche 400, powered by an eight- cylinder Lycoming IO-720 engine pumping out 400hp. They also might talk to you about the two-engine version—the Twin Comanche.

Also, the US government, in the guise of the FAA, will help you along with some information in pamphlet form about what to look for when considering a general aviation airplane. The pamphlet is called *Plane Sense* and can be obtained by writing: US Department of Transportation, Federal Aviation Administration, Aviation Standards National Field Office, Examinations Standards Branch, AVN-130, PO Box 25082, Oklahoma City, OK 73125.

Ask them for advisory circular AC-20-5f, dated 1986. For once, it's an item of paperwork from the government that you can actually read in plain English. The Feds do a good job of translating aviation-speak into real English in the circular, making it much easier to understand.

Now that I am a little older and the top part of me has less hair, I don't spend as much time flying as I do word-processing, and my aviation needs have changed with the years. In the past twenty years I've been to some pretty interesting places, flown some interesting airplanes, but most of all met some real interesting people. I've also learned a little about airplanes, and that's what this book is all about. So sit down, get comfortable, turn up the light, put *Top Gun* in the video for later, and enjoy yourself while I tell you stories about Mr. Piper's airplanes.

The Rating System

All the airplanes in this book are rated in three categories using numbers 1 through 5 (1 being the most desirable and 5 being the least desirable).

The categories are Investment, Utility, and Popularity. Each airplane will be rated from one to five:

#1—A sure investment. It will appreciate in value and is highly popular.

#2—An ok investment; the airplane has appreciated, but not as much as those in category #1. It is fairly popular or popular for certain purposes.

#3—An average airplane. Probably won't appreciate, but won't depreciate either. It is a good airplane, just not outstanding in any category.

#4—A depreciating airplane. It's probably not going to make you any money, and it's not real well known or popular. The cost to operate the airplane may outweigh its value. The engines might constitute 80–90 percent of the airplane's value. Your money is better spent elsewhere.

#5—Not a recommended purchase. For a specific reason, it's not a good airplane. Expect to buy a money pit with high operating costs relative to return.

Remember, however, that these ratings are based on opinions of pilots I've interviewed and on my own experiences. If you have found the airplane of your dreams, far be it from me to dissuade you from owning it. This is only a *guide* to Piper airplanes—nothing in it is engraved in stone.

The airplane flight manual approved by the FAA is the official source of operating parameters and performance information. The performance information in this book assumes an airplane with a certain amount of factory-installed equipment flown under standard atmospheric conditions at sea level, and should not be considered applicable to other situations. In planning each flight, I urge you to allow for a comfortable reserve.

All information contained in this book is based on the latest data available at the time of publication. All specifications are subject to change without prior notice. All models of Piper aircraft can be discontinued as required.

Chapter 1

The Classics

Cub and Cruiser

The Piper Aircraft Corporation began production of aircraft in Lock Haven, Pennsylvania, in 1937. The company had been formed from the ashes of the Taylor Aircraft Company after the Taylor factory at Bradford, Pennsylvania, was destroyed by fire.

Piper Aircraft Corporation's first aircraft, the J-3 Cub, introduced in 1937, was a simple airplane, with a 40hp Continental or Franklin

About 75 percent of all World War II pilots attended aviation kindergarten in a J-3 Cub. Many, many thousands were built—5,000 before the war even started, another 5,000 during the war as the L-4 observation and liaison aircraft. There are still plenty around, some flying, others in decay. The J-3 is the prototypical rag-wing taildragger: 22ft long, 35ft wing span, 80mph cruise. A three-seat version, the PA-11 Super Cruiser, was also built in large numbers and is still fairly popular; the Super Cruiser, with fully enclosed engine, has a rated 100mph cruise. A rare version, the J-4, has a modified tail and wheel spats. Tucked in amongst all the modern singles and light twins is this 50-year-old J-3, still clean and airworthy on a Saturday afternoon. The one concession to the passage of time (and airport requirements) is a hand-held radio strapped to the frame.

engine. Later Cubs were fitted with 50hp or 65hp Continental, Franklin, or Lycoming engines.

This advertisement appeared in popular magazines during World War II and may have had something to do with the explosive growth of general aviation following the war.

The J-3 Cub was built from Sitka spruce and chrome-moly tubing covered with Grade A cotton fabric, treated with nitrate dope on the early models, butyrate dope being used on the post WWII Cubs. The early wing spars were framed in spruce up to 1941, when Piper found it had $40,000, in 1940s dollars, worth of wing spars that couldn't pass CAA (pre-FAA) inspection. From then on, Piper put dural (a type of aluminum alloy) spars on all its rag-wing airplanes.

By the late thirties, Luscombe, Funk, Aeronca, Taylorcraft, and Rearwin all had certificated airplanes up to 75hp. Piper didn't want to be left behind with no airplane to sell while all the other companies made money, so they introduced the J-4 Cub Coupe in 1938.

Initially hooked to a 50hp Continental engine sporting an 1,800hr TBO, the Coupe grew through 65hp to a final 75hp engine, still enjoying the same TBO. It came equipped

Cub and Cruiser Rating
Investment: #1
Utility: #1
Popularity: #1 (If you're a Cub Crazy)

Well, here we are, ready for the active. When this plane was new, headsets were sissy stuff. There are supposed to be 65hp ready to work inside those four cylinders hanging out in the slipstream.

J-4 Cub Specifications
Engine: Continental A-50-1, 50hp at 1,900rpm
Maximum Weight: 1,200lb
Fuel Capacity: 16gal
Maximum Speed: 93mph
Cruise Speed: 83mph
Fuel Consumption: 3.6gph
Range: 325 miles
Rate of Climb at Sea Level: 480fpm
Service Ceiling: 10,500ft
Stall Speed: 35mph
Standard Empty Weight: 710lb
Maximum Useful Load: 490lb
Wing Span: 36.12ft
Length: 22.5ft
Height: 82in

J-4-E Specifications
Engine: Continental A-75, 75hp at 2,600rpm
Maximum Weight: 1,400lb
Fuel Capacity: 25gal
Maximum Speed: 105mph
Cruise Speed: 96mph
Fuel Consumption: 4.9gph
Range: 460 miles
Rate of Climb at Sea Level: 600fpm
Service Ceiling: 12,000ft
Stall Speed: 40mph
Standard Empty Weight: 865lb
Maximum Useful Load: 535lb
Wing Span: 36.12ft
Length: 22.5ft
Height: 82in

with dual ignition and a starter on the bigger engine, which was a change for the good, after having to hand-prop the earlier planes.

Standard equipment on this side-by-side two-seater included such items as built-in radio, indirectly lit instruments, compensated compass, full-swivel tailwheel, clock, battery and navigation lights, a cabin heater (considering that all that separated you from the elements was a piece of fabric similar to a bed sheet, the heater meant a lot), hydraulic brakes including parking brake, and a muffler. The coupe sat two people on a common seat, a baggage compartment capable of carrying 105lb mounted behind.

The standard fuel supply of 25gal, 16gal in the right wing, 9gal in the left, gave the

75hp Coupe a range of more than 450 miles. Back in 1939, this was quite a range for a light airplane.

The 75hp Coupe had a stainless steel exhaust muffler on the engine. The whole nose

Off we go! The Cub, like most others of its generation of primary trainers, really didn't need a runway. As my first flight instructor used to demonstrate, the taxiway at our highly uncontrolled airport was perfectly suitable, and you could just about launch straight out of the parking spot if you wanted. Times have changed, however, and these birdmen are behaving themselves and observing the rules.

J-4-A Specifications
Engine: Continental A-65, 65hp at 1,900rpm
Maximum Weight: 1,300lb
Fuel Capacity: 25gal
Maximum Speed: 100mph
Cruise Speed: 92mph
Fuel Consumption: 4.2gph
Range: 460 miles
Rate of Climb at Sea Level: 600fpm
Service Ceiling: 12,000ft
Stall Speed: 37mph
Standard Empty Weight: 740lb
Maximum Useful Load: 560lb
Wing Span: 36.12ft
Length: 22.5ft
Height: 82in

The 90hp Super Cub hit the airplane market in 1949, a worthy successor to a long line of Cubs going back to 1931. More than 40,000 Cubs have been built, over the years. The current Super Cub, with its 150hp Lycoming powerplant, will fly circles around the older versions. The aircraft stayed in production until 1982 and over 30,000 were built.

The PA-18 Super Cub design is really a modernized J-3, with metal replacing wood for some major structural components and a more powerful engine. After Piper ceased production, a Texas company picked up the design, offering the old Cub for the approximate sticker price of what B-24s used to cost.

The PA-18 Super Cub has become the quintessential fabric-covered taildragger and remains not only extremely popular and pricey, but is still in production. There are very few airplanes that, for whatever reason, accomplish their mission so well that they stay in production fifty years after they were designed, but the Cub is one—maybe the only one.

J-4 F Specifications
Engine: Lycoming O-145, 55hp at 2,300rpm
Maximum Weight: 1,200lb
Fuel Capacity: 16gal
Maximum Speed: 95mph
Cruise Speed: 85mph
Fuel Consumption: 3.8gph
Range: 340 miles
Rate of Climb at Sea Level: 540fpm
Service Ceiling: 11,000ft
Stall Speed: 35mph
Standard Empty Weight: 720lb
Maximum Useful Load: 480lb
Wing Span: 36.12ft
Length: 22.5ft
Height: 82in

J-5A-75 and J-5B-75 Specifications
Engine: Continental A-75-8, 75hp at 2,600rpm; or
  Lycoming GO-145, 75hp at 3,200rpm
Maximum Weight: 1,450lb
Fuel Capacity: 25gal
Maximum Speed: 95mph
Cruise Speed at 3,000ft: 80mph
Range: 380 miles
Rate of Climb at Sea Level: 400fpm
Service Ceiling: 13,000ft
Stall Speed: 43mph
Standard Empty Weight: 820lb
Maximum Useful Load: 630lb
Wing Span: 35.5ft
Length: 22.5ft
Height: 82in

of the airplane was covered by a cowling with stainless steel grilles over the air intakes. Automobile styling of the time was clearly evident in the airplane.

The Coupe retailed for $1,995, but extras such as wheel pants, pontoons, and skis cost extra. A parachute—silk no less—was on the option list for $225.

The J-5 Cub Cruiser was advertised in 1940 as "priced hundreds of dollars lower than the next lowest-priced three-placed ship." It was flown solo from the front, two passengers in the rear seat. Piper showed some early photographs of the Cruiser, seating three 165lb men in the cabin. They all were smiling, so it must have been a comfortable ride even with a 37in wide rear seat. With all three aboard, takeoff run was less than 500ft. Quite an accomplishment for an airplane with 75hp and 1,450lb gross weight.

Here's a Super Cub chugging along at cruise, a whopping 115mph, down low where it won't get in the way of more modern airplanes. The design uses a constant-chord, rounded-tip, braced high wing and is readily distinguished from earlier Cubs by the enclosed cylinders and the landing light and air intake below the spinner (both lacking in J-3s and Cruisers).

Dual controls allowed its use as a trainer, or it could be changed to a passenger airplane in less than 15sec: two retractable foot rests prevented rear seat passengers from interfering with the rudder pedals, and the aft stick was removable. The J-5B was introduced in 1941 with a geared, 75hp Lycoming engine.

The J-5C was introduced in 1942 with a 100hp Lycoming engine. The J-5C's frame was built from chrome-moly steel, as had been all the other rag-wing Pipers to that time. Chrome-moly steel is lighter and stronger than mild steel tubing. It does require some specialized welding techniques, though, requiring normalizing prior to use to keep it from suffering from hydrogen embrittlement.

The J-5C came with one door on the right side and was fitted out with an aft deck that could be raised to accommodate two stretchers. Eighteen gallons of fuel came standard in the right wing, feeding a 2gal tank behind the engine. Seven- or 18gal tanks were optional in the left wing. The J-5C came with all the same optional equipment as the Coupe.

Approximately 900 Cruisers were manufactured from 1940, until civilian production

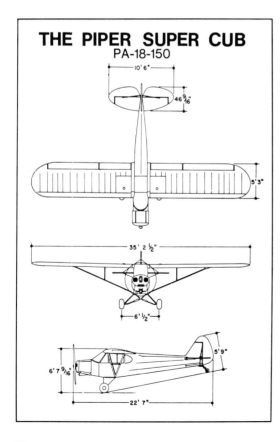

THE PIPER SUPER CUB
PA-18-150

was halted by the need for wartime production.

The US Navy, seeing a need for a liaison plane that could double as an ambulance, ordered 100 of the J-5C Cruisers modified with a hinged turtledeck that lifted to allow two litters to be carried. The Navy called their new air ambulance the HE-1. Sometime later, the Navy redesignated these aircraft AE-1.

The Cruiser went to war with the Army in 1942, as did the J-3 Cub, which was called the L-4 or O-59. At one time, Piper was producing military J-3 Cubs at a rate of one every ten minutes. They served in all theaters of operation, filling a multitude of roles. They shuffled brass from hither to yon, acted as an airborne ambulance, and hauled cargo—all the jobs helicopters would do in the future.

In WWII the Army Air Force took delivery of 4,800 Piper liaison airplanes of various designations and horsepowers. The Civilian

Pilot Training Program, begun in 1939, later changed to the War Training service, used over 10,000 airplanes in its program, over 80 percent of its pilots gaining their wings in Piper J-3 Cubs. The military Cubs saw service as diversified as mail delivery and artillery spotter, many coming back to land with battle damage or bullet holes. All the military orders were canceled at the cessation of hostilities in the Pacific.

After the war ended, Piper resumed production of light airplanes in early 1946 with the three-place Super Cruiser. It was the same basic airplane as the 1942 J-5C with a few extras, and 3,800 had been built when production ended in 1948. A 19gal fuel tank came standard on the right wing, another similar sized tank was offered as an option for the left. It was a typical chrome-moly fuselage and dural wing spar airplane, covered with fabric. Gross weight was 1,750lb, but it could

There are lots of Cubs of all kinds around; over 30,000 were manufactured and many can be seen leaping from the concrete of airports everywhere on any Saturday morning, using almost none of the available runway. They offer a particular kind of flying experience that is probably quite impractical for most of us, while being equally fun and instructive. This is the antithesis of the fast, heavy, expensive, high-capacity twin that earns its keep. Current average price is $50,000.

PA-11-65 Specifications
Engine: Continental A-65-8/9, 65hp at 2,300rpm
Maximum Weight: 1,220lb
Fuel Capacity: 18gal
Maximum Speed: 100mph
Cruise Speed: 87mph at 3,000ft
Range: 300 miles
Fuel Consumption: 4.7gph
Rate of Climb at Sea Level: 514fpm
Service Ceiling: 14,000ft
Ground Run: 350ft
Stall Speed: 38mph
Standard Empty Weight: 730lb
Maximum Useful Load: 490lb
Wing Span: 35.25ft
Wing Area: 178.5sq-ft
Length: 22.4ft
Height: 80in

be flown in limited aerobatics at a 250lb lighter weight.

After the war, Piper moved the J-3's fuel tank to the left wing, installed a full cowl over the engine, bumped the horsepower to 90 with a Continental C-90 (1,800hr TBO), and called it the PA-11 (PA= Piper Airplane, the new nomenclature). The biggest noticeable difference between the PA-11 and the J-3 was that the J-3 soloed from the rear seat, while the PA-11 pilot flew from the front.

Towards the end of 1947, Piper came out with the PA-14 Family Cruiser, a descendant of the J-5. It was touted as "the world's lowest

PA-11-90 Specifications
Engine: Continental C-90, 90hp at 2,475rpm, 1,800hr TBO
Maximum Weight: 1,220lb
Fuel Capacity: 18gal
Maximum Speed: 112mph
Cruise Speed: 100mph
Range: 350 miles
Fuel Consumption: 5gph
Rate of Climb at Sea Level: 900fpm
Service Ceiling: 16,000ft
Stall Speed: 40mph
Standard Empty Weight: 750lb
Maximum Useful Load: 470lb
Wing Span: 35.25ft
Wing Area: 178.5sq-ft
Length: 22.4ft
Height: 80in

priced four-place plane." Only 237 were built due to the sales slump going on at that time. The Family Cruiser was 4in wider to make room for the fourth seat. If all seats were filled, everybody had to be good friends, enjoying a seat width of only 41in as they did. At the same time, it picked up a 100lb increase in gross weight over the Super Cruiser. A 108hp Lycoming was hung on the front. This was not a lot of horsepower for a 1,850lb gross, four-seat airplane, but Piper was trying to keep costs under $4,000.

The airplane we are most familiar with, the Super Cub, was first certified in 1949. Power started at 90hp and grew through 108hp and 125hp to the final 150hp Super Cub that was in production in kit form and as a finished airplane into 1991. The last kits sold in the $50,000 range—a lot of money for an airplane first priced at $7,880.

The Super Cub has seen just about every kind of landing gear one could imagine. One Cub, assigned to duty at the North Pole, was fitted with 36in-tall, low pressure "tundra tires," enabling it to operate out of places that could only loosely be defined as airstrips. Edo floats were fitted to some Super Cubs, opening up many inaccessible areas far from roads. When the floats were checked off on the option list, the frame was painted with zinc chromate by the factory to help prevent salt-water corrosion.

If your destination involved snow, skis attached to the wheels let you land in any kind of winter country from prairies to glaciers. Once the airplane had come to a stop, the skis could be retracted above the wheels. This kept them from freezing to the ice, making movement all but impossible. Sounds like one of those lessons learned the hard way.

Imagine returning to your airplane after a brisk three-hour stroll in -40deg weather, just to find the airplane stuck to the ice along the entire length of the skis. After having hours of fun cutting them free, someone came up with the idea of rigging the skis so they could be picked up above the tires while stopped on ice or snow. That way, only the tires had to be broken loose from the ice when it was time to go.

Trying to think of all the uses that a Cub has been put to is like trying to count ants.

The handsome J-5 Cruiser was powered by a 75hp Continental (or Lycoming, if you wished) engine and offered Spartan accommodations for three, the pilot up front and a bench seat for two small, friendly people astern. The J-5 was announced in 1940, and Piper built almost 500 of them before the year was out. Another 870 went out the door in 1941, but the war cut production to a trickle and only about 60 were made in 1942. The Army bought one variant, the YL-14 with a 125hp engine, in small quantities. J-5C Cruisers were fitted with 100hp engines. *Pete Bowers*

Every time you think you're through, another one pops up. The Cub and its newer versions have been used for powerline, pipeline, and border patrol, and many other purposes. Whether on wheels, floats, or skis, the Cub is a go-anywhere, do-everything method of transportation.

A friend of mine flew one in Montana all year around to check his stock. He says that once he got caught in a "white out," where he couldn't make out the horizon. Earth and sky looked all the same to him. He pulled the power back to a slow walk and let the airplane down in 50ft increments. When he and his altimeter said the ground must be somewhere right below him, he put the Cub into a very shallow right turn, then tossed out an orange hunting vest that had been wadded under the front seat. He said it didn't fall too far before it hit the snow. With the vest as a guide he was able to set up a real short approach and land. Personally, I prefer to stick to sunny days and 20-mile visibility.

So what hurdles do you have to jump when buying a Cub? Most of the pre-fifties Piper Cruisers and J-4 and J-5 series Coupes are becoming quite rare because some of the airplanes were made in numbers less than 100. Going through The Cub Club (P.O. Box 2002, Mt. Pleasant, MI 48804) or The Piper Owner Society (P.O. Box 337, Iola, WI 54945) will be one of the better ways to find Cubs and Cruisers manufactured prior to 1950. The Experimental Aircraft Association (EAA, EAA Aviation Center, Oshkosh, WI 54903) is also a good source of information and parts.

When looking at older Cubs and any other Piper with wood wings, a proper inspection is especially important. Wood rots if kept wet for any length of time. When inspecting an airplane with wood wings, you want to make sure all the drain holes are open. Check for moisture under any metal fittings. Look at the low points of the wing where moisture would collect. If any of the visible wood shows any discoloration, use an ice pick or similar instrument to probe for rot. Most bad areas can be cut out and replaced by people who have lots of experience in working on wood airplanes.

The chrome-moly frame will rust rapidly if the bare metal is left exposed for as short as 24hr. Any minor repairs should be covered on the outside with a metal protector like zinc chromate primer or Stits Epoxy. At one time, linseed oil was flowed through the inside of the frame to keep rust from forming. It's worked pretty well for the last fifty years or so, but now there are other types of chemicals capable of doing a better job; Stits Tubeseal for one.

Rusted parts of the frame will have to be cut out, new pieces welded in place and treated with a rust inhibitor. Drill a small hole at the top of the repair about one inch from the end. The inhibitor can then be injected into the frame.

This job is one better left to a mechanic with lots of experience on rag-wing-and-tubing airplanes, because it requires an ability to repair chrome-moly only gained with years of practice. If welded improperly, chrome-moly has a bad tendency to break just behind the weld. Having this happen at 3,500ft would really ruin your day.

Some of the Piper J-4s and Cruisers that signed up for the duration during WWII have been restored as military airplanes. If you lust in your heart for any of these "Warbugs" be aware that military history won't make an airplane fly any better, but it will make it fly more expensively. Any liaison or observation Piper will cost considerably more than its civilian counterpart. Having a good working knowledge and some time in the air in the type of airplane that you're interested in owning will be more help than just reading a book. Go to a few antique shows at your nearby airport, talk to some owners about what they went through restoring their airplanes. I highly doubt that any of them will hesitate to tell you more about their airplane than you thought you would ever want to learn. Some gas money might even get you a ride or two. The easiest way to learn about them is to go look at them.

A 1947 Super Cruiser, fully restored, is currently in the paper for $29,500 OBO. Is it a good deal? Well, another is listed at $35,000, everything show condition. Then there's the one with a cracked crankshaft—$15,000. A good 1981 Super Cub will bring $60,000. The highest priced Super Cub in *Trade-A-Plane* is being offered in September 1993 for $78,000. It comes with everything, including autopilot and King IFR (instrument flight rules) navigation equipment. Seems to me like putting a custom saddle on a donkey. Will they bring their asking price? Hard to say. Any of the old Cubs in restored condition will be collectors items, most likely to be found at antique airshows sporting modern prices.

Vagabond

Both the PA-15 and the PA-17 were introduced within months of each other in 1948, and 700, of which 500 were PA-15s and the balance PA-17s, were built by the time production ceased in 1950. A $200 price difference between the two Vagabonds seemed to be enough to keep people away from the more expensive PA-17.

The PA-15 was the budget model: if it wasn't necessary for flight, it probably wasn't in the airplane. You were lucky to get a seat and stick. A two-placer, it departed from previous tandem seating by placing both people side-by-side. Only the left side had flight controls, though. It was equipped with brakes, but not enough engine to get going really fast to need them. PA-15 performance could be said to be a bit anemic. A 65hp Lycoming O-145 hid under the cowl, but where the horses were hiding was anybody's guess. Cruise, advertised at 90mph, was only obtained with a new engine and light load. The best part of the PA-15 was its $1,995 price and its low fuel consumption.

The standard Cub wing, with 3ft missing from the inboard side, was used on both Vagabonds, making them the first "short-wing" Pipers; a process that would be continued on future models.

PA-15 Specifications
Engine: Lycoming O-145, 65hp at 2,550rpm
Maximum Weight: 1,100lb
Fuel Capacity: 12gal
Maximum Speed: 100mph
Cruise Speed: 90mph
Range: 250 miles
Rate of Climb at Sea Level: 510fpm
Service Ceiling: 10,000ft
Stall Speed: 45mph (with flaps)
Standard Empty Weight: 630lb
Wing Span: 29.3ft
Length: 18.7ft
Height: 72in

A 12gal fuel tank was mounted in front of the windshield, a trick that any aircraft manufacturer would be hard pressed to get away with today. Imagine having your fuel tank as the first thing to arrive at the scene of an accident. The lawyers would rub their hands and cackle with glee.

For the extra $200, you could have moved up to a PA-17. It came with the Continental A-65 engine, with a real 65hp turning a Mc Cauley metal prop. Other than a slightly greater rate of climb, the PA-17 POH shows the same performance as the PA-15, but the PA-17 outshown its cheaper twin.

For the extra expense, the PA-17 came with a few more amenities like dual controls, floor mats, flight instruments, and engine gauges. If you chipped in a few dollars more, a 6gal auxiliary fuel tank could be had.

A lot of the Vagabonds that still exist have had their 65hp engines replaced by something with a lot more power, usually in the 108-125hp range. This greatly improves all aspects of performance on what was a relatively underpowered airplane in the first place.

A Vagabond PA-15, with 2,600hr TT, 130hr since rebuild, is being offered as having been fully restored in 1986, with many modern updates, for $16,000. The ad says it is like new and the Stits fabric shows no wear. A

You could get a cute little Vagabond like this, factory fresh and with a 65hp Lycoming, for only $1,990 back in 1948. The Vagabond was the first of the short-wing breed, and came in two variants, the PA-15 (a simple, stripped model) and the PA-17 (the deluxe package, $2,195). You can still find the Vagabond, but you have to pay more for it now. They are rare—only about 500 were built. *Pete Bowers*

This PA-16 Clipper is powered by a 115hp Lycoming O-235. The Clipper was a bigger version of the Vagabond, with seating for four. In the unlikely event that you find one of these PA-16s for sale, it will have been built around 1950. Current prices are around $15,000 for one in good condition, about $19,000 for something more pristine. *Pete Bowers*

PA-17 Specifications
Engine: Continental A-65, 65hp at 2,300rpm
Maximum Weight: 1,150lb
Fuel Capacity: 12gal
Maximum Speed: 100mph
Cruise Speed: 90mph
Range: 250 miles
Rate of Climb at Sea Level: 530fpm
Service Ceiling: 10,500ft
Stall Speed: 45mph
Standard Empty Weight: 650lb
Wing Span: 29.3ft
Length: 18.7ft
Height: 72in

number of "projects" are available for less than $8,000; however, you should be careful about tackling a full restoration, unless you had done something similar in the past as there's always more work involved than apparent at first glance. Should you be bargain hunting, try to pick one that is at least flying—restore it as you go.

Clipper and Pacer

The PA-16 Clipper was an interim airplane, produced only during 1949; 726 being completed before the Pacer was introduced. A total of 726 were produced before its discontinuation at the end of the year. The Clipper was, more or less, a Vagabond with four seats, 36gal fuel tanks, and the same poor brakes that could get you in trouble on landing—punishing any lack of attention with a ground loop. Combined with the narrowness of the landing gear, the tendency to swap ends made for some exciting rides for pilots new to the airplane.

The Clipper was the first of the "short-wing," four-seat Pipers. For more information on this airplane and all the other "short-wings" contact The Short Wing Piper Club, P.O. Box 66, Collinsville, OK 74021.

It wasn't really powerful enough for a four-place single; 115hp and a gross of 1,600lb limiting climb rate on a hot day to 25fpm. More power was clearly needed.

Clipper and Pacer Rating
Investment: #3
Utility: #4
Popularity: #3

The PA-20 Pacer was in production for two years, starting in 1950, and over 1,100 were sold. The very first had 115hp Lycomings, but most later versions had 125hp engines and a few had 135hp powerplants and variable-pitch propellers installed. *Pete Bowers*

In 1950 the power problem was alleviated somewhat by the introduction of the 125hp Piper PA-20 Pacer. In 1949, Piper began delivering a Lycoming O-290-D powered, four-seat airplane, built along the same "rag-and-tube" construction of the earlier planes. As many as 1,100 were built before Piper shifted production totally over to the Tri-Pacer in 1952.

Later in the Pacer production run, the Lycoming 135hp engine and the Aeromatic, semi-constant-speed propeller became available. This engine gave a 125mph cruise speed over 580 miles—which was a 13mph increase in speed and a 100-mile increase in range over the Clipper, and the Pacer could do all this carrying a 100lb higher useful load of 930lb.

Personally, of all the fifties airplanes, I prefer the Pacer with the 135hp engine and Aeromatic "constant-speed" propeller options. The prop is not a true constant-speed prop, rather its adjustable counterweights can be set on the ground to change the cruise pitch. Of all the Pacers and Clippers, this gives the best overall performance, coupled with the highest useful load, making it a real four-person, cross-country airplane.

The Pacer was the first rag-wing to be fitted like the newer Piper models. Flaps, front and rear doors, twin fuel tanks, and basic instruments (no vacuum system—no directional gyro [DG] or attitude indicator [AI]—although there are Supplemental Type Certificates, STCs, available for addition of a venturi horn to drive those instruments) were stan-

---

PA-16 Specifications

Engine: Lycoming O-235-C1, 115hp at 2,800rpm
Maximum Weight: 1,650lb
Fuel Capacity: 36gal
Maximum Speed: 125mph
Cruise Speed: 112mph
Fuel Consumption: 7gph
Range: 480 miles
Rate of Climb at Sea Level: 600fpm
Service Ceiling: 11,000ft
Stall Speed: 50mph
Standard Empty Weight: 850lb
Maximum Useful Load: 600lb (with full tanks)
Wing Span: 29.25ft
Length: 20.1ft
Height: 74in

```
PA-20-125 Specifications
Engine: Lycoming O-290-D, 125hp at 2,600rpm
Maximum Weight: 1,850lb
Fuel Capacity: 36gal
Maximum Speed: 135mph
Cruise 75% Power at Sea Level: 125mph
Fuel Consumption: 7.3gph
Range: 580 miles
Rate of Climb at Sea Level: 810fpm
Service Ceiling: 14,250ft
Takeoff Run: 1,372ft
Landing Roll: 500ft
Stall Speed: 48mph
Standard Empty Weight: 970lb
Maximum Useful Load: 830lb
Wing Span: 29.3ft
Length: 20.4ft
Height: 74.5in
```

dard, although a radio was not part of the package. It had to be optioned later, as in the newer Pipers.

As the years progressed, many STCs became available for the PA-16 and PA-20. Some of the more common are: a change to a Maule tailwheel—giving increased steering capability; stronger wing-strut fittings—Jensen fittings (from any shop) which are double the diameter of stock parts that had a bad tendency of rusting through; gross weight increase (PA-20 only) from 1,800lb to 1,950lb (this is only for the 125hp Pacer); and a venturi vacuum horn.

```
Pacer PA-20-135 Specifications
Engine: Lycoming O-290-D2, 135hp at 2,600rpm
Maximum Weight: 1,950lb
Fuel Capacity: 36gal
Maximum Speed: 139mph
Cruise Speed: 125mph
Fuel Consumption: 8gph
Range: 580 miles
Rate of Climb at Sea Level: 620fpm
Service Ceiling: 15,000ft
Takeoff Run: 1,220ft (flaps extended)
Landing Roll: 500ft (flaps extended)
Stall Speed: 48mph (flaps extended)
Standard Empty Weight: 1,020lb
Maximum Useful Load: 930lb
Wing Span: 29.3ft
Length: 20.4ft
Height: 74.5in
```

Perusing the publications, I found one PA-16, with King radio, transponder, and intercom, listed for $12,750. A 1949 Clipper, pitched as totally restored, was listed for $18,500. The only Pacer I was able to locate had less than 3,000hr on the tach, newer fabric, paint, and interior, and a modern center stack of radios, all for only $22,000. A little high in my book, but here again, price on the older Pipers is strictly driven by aircraft condition. This Pacer just might be worth the money. The only way to tell is to go take a look and a ride in the airplane.

Be prepared to pay for the fuel used in any demo ride, as the owner, like others, isn't in the business of giving free rides to tire kickers. One of the ways to show that you're serious about buying an airplane is to offer to cover some of the expenses involved in transfer of ownership. If you can't afford to pay for some fuel and the cost of a pre-purchase inspection, you're surely going to have trouble paying the tariff on operating the airplane. Come prepared to spend some cash. Might as well learn from the start that the one thing that makes airplanes fly is *money*.

Tri-Pacer

Someone at Piper thought they would make a daring move and shift the tailwheel of the Pacer up to the front of the airplane. The sales department took the idea and advertised it as the airplane that "anyone can fly." Once people found out how much easier it was to fly an airplane with tricycle gear, sales of the Tri-Pacer fast outran those of the tailwheel Pacer. Other than the Super Cub, Piper hasn't built any taildraggers since 1960.

The Tri-Pacer enjoyed a nine-year production run, and 7,600 were built during that time. The early models had a Lycoming O-290-D engine for 125hp; by 1959 this had changed to an O-320-B Lycoming rated at 160hp. The Tri-Pacer's 36gal of fuel allow a cross-country range of 500 miles at 9gph.

The brakes were actuated by a long "Johnson Bar" below the center of the panel, operating both left and right brakes together. Toe brakes weren't fitted to the rudder pedals except as an aftermarket STC. The trim is literally cranked in by use of an overhead crank resembling a window winder off a 1952

Chevrolet. Turn it one way, the nose goes up. Reverse the direction, the nose drops.

Takeoffs and landings are standard Piper tricycle gear operations—very docile. Full throttle, a little rudder to offset torque, off you lift at 60mph. A climb rate of 800fpm brings up 90mph on the airspeed indicator, a good speed to climb up to cruising altitude.

As far as power-off glides, the Tri-Pacer behaves similarly to all the other short-wing Pipers. With power back at idle, 80mph or more must be carried to keep the sink rate from increasing past 1,000fpm.

Landings are quite easy, no bad habits whatsoever. Hold the nose up until the main wheels touch and lightly apply the brakes. Landings are nothing like those in the Tri-Pacer's taildragger relatives.

In some aviation circles, if you can't fly a tailwheel airplane, then you're not truly a pilot. When I was young, dumb, and just starting out in the airplane ownership business, I had the opportunity to make numerous trips to Mexico. At the time, I owned a

1967 Piper Cherokee 140. Not a real fire breather, but it got my second ex-wife-to-be and I around Mexico. We went as far south as Tapachula, which is within mango-throwing distance of Guatemala. As the thought of getting shot at didn't appeal to me at the time, we elected not to go any farther south. Guatemala Radio, on 126.9, was issuing notices stating that "anyone entering within 200 miles of Guatemalan airspace without prior permission would be fired on without warning." 'Nuff for me. I'll stay in Mexico.

Most of the time the Cherokee covered the ground at a little over 100kt. Not blazing performance, but it was a vacation and we were running on *manana* time. If we got some-

The PA-20 Pacer gave way to the PA-22 Tri-Pacer in 1952 and was produced for over eight years, before giving way in turn to the Colt variant which lasted another three years. The Tri-Pacer, in the grand Piper tradition, made incremental improvements on the previous model, the PA-20 Pacer, which donated its airframe to the project. Tri-Pacers got much more powerful engines, though, and sticker prices to match. Toward the end of the production run, in 1960, you could drop $10,000 on a Super Custom Tri-Pacer with full panel and 160hp engine. Current prices are in that vicinity, about $10,000 to $15,000.

PA-22-125 Specifications

Engine: Lycoming O-290-D, 125hp at 2,600rpm, 2,000hr TBO
Maximum Weight: 1,800lb
Fuel Capacity: 36gal
Maximum Speed: 133mph
Cruise Speed: 123mph
Fuel Consumption: 7.7gph
Range: 580 miles
Rate of Climb at Sea Level: 810fpm
Service Ceiling: 14,250ft
Takeoff Run: 1,372ft
Landing Roll: 500ft
Stall Speed: 48mph (flaps extended)
Standard Empty Weight: 1,000lb
Maximum Useful Load: 800lb
Wing Span: 29.3ft
Length: 20.4ft
Height: 100in

where tomorrow, that was ok. If we got there next week, that was ok too.

After that trip, we started traveling with a group of pilots who flew mostly taildraggers of the Cessna 180 and 185 variety. After a while I got tired of dragging up the rest of the show; being last on the field by 30min. I decided to go play macho taildragger owner, selling the Cherokee and buying a 1955 Cessna 180. Boy did my education in airplanes begin. First, getting insurance required 15hr

PA-22-160 Specifications

Engine: Lycoming O-320-B, 160hp at 2,700rpm, 2,000hr TBO
Maximum Weight: 2,000lb
Fuel Capacity: 36gal
Maximum Speed: 141mph
Cruise Speed: 125mph
Fuel Consumption: 9gph
Range: 500 miles
Rate of Climb at Sea Level: 800fpm
Service Ceiling: 16,500ft
Takeoff Run: 1,120ft (flaps extended)
Landing Roll: 500ft (flaps extended)
Stall Speed: 49mph (flaps extended)
Standard Empty Weight: 1,110lb
Maximum Useful Load: 890lb
Wing Span: 29.3ft
Length: 20.6ft
Height: 100in

of instruction before the company would even talk about coverage.

I needed all fifteen. The instructor must have gone to the Marquis de Sade school of flight instruction. We landed in places that only resembled runways because an airplane was already on the ground. He took me into grass strips less than 1,500ft long. With big trees at the end. We worked out of an unimproved dirt strip right under a Terminal Control Area (TCA). I *learned* how to fly a taildragger.

What did I gain when it came to real flying? Well, I learned how to sweat profusely when the outside temperature is 40deg with a 15kt crosswind on the runway. I found out that I could not quit flying the airplane until it was tied down. I could do some neat tricks in the airplane like pull 45deg of flaps, point the nose downhill and coast down at 80mph, hit the numbers on the runway and have to add power to taxi to the first turn-off. But I never learned how to land that airplane without getting dry-mouth. Once I moved into a Cherokee Six, all those problems disappeared. Maybe I'm not much of a taildragger pilot, that's ok. Besides, if taildraggers were a good idea, aircraft manufacturers would still be building them. Imagine a Boeing 747 taildragger!

Anyway, Piper's shift to tricycle geared airplanes in 1952 was one of their better ideas. From the first 125hp Lycoming O-290, the Tri-Pacer moved up to a 135hp O-290 in 1952, then to a 150hp O-320 in 1955. The final power option was the 160hp Lycoming O-320, offered in 1958.

The Tri-Pacer is the last tube and fabric airplane built by Piper. They can be inexpensive to purchase, but costly to maintain if the fabric needs to be replaced. A good fabric like Stits or Airtex Re-cover envelopes can last up to ten years with good care. Keep the airplane clean and polished; look for a hangar to hide it from the sun. If it must sit out, protective wing covers can keep the sun from eating the fabric.

Finding a Tri-Pacer shouldn't be too difficult. A mere $15,000–20,000 ought to buy just about any rebuilt, recovered, and re-engined Tri-Pacer on the market. The *N.A.D.A. Retail Aircraft Appraisal Guide* for the first third of 1993 shows the last year Tri-Pacer, 1960, with a low value of $17,800; the average resale is $20,500; high book runs $25,800. Looking at early models, the 1952 model shows a low of $9,500; average retail is $11,400; a fully restored airplane brings a high of $14,400.

With the market for airplanes continually fluctuating, it would be wise to use these prices as guides only. Relative prices between two different airplanes will probably still stay the same, but where actual dollar amounts will settle is hard to predict.

Colt

The PA-22 Colt is the Tri-Pacer with 108hp and two seats. It will carry two people over 600 miles without refueling, however, 100mph is about all the faster you will go. For an older, slightly underpowered airplane, it makes good transportation for a couple looking to enjoy flying more than covering a lot of ground quickly.

Piper built around 1,800 Colts from 1960 to 1963, so locating one will take more work than finding a Tri-Pacer. However, they are to be found with a little work. If you like the Tri-Pacer and Colt look, and don't mind working on fabric-covered airplanes, either one would be a good first airplane. The technology has existed for over 60 years. The airplanes are quite simple (if you disagree, go look under the panel of a Mooney 231). Repairs and annuals won't send you out looking for a second job. And you will definitely meet some interesting people as you get to know your airplane a little better.

This two-place airplane was offered in three models; Standard, Custom, and Super Custom. The options added to the basic airplane—radio, more instruments, and auxiliary fuel tanks—determined the model. Today almost all the Colts around have been updated with modern radios, so the different models really don't matter as much. The

The old and the new: a pristine J-3 glitters off the runway in flashy Cub yellow, behind the majestic buzz of 65 little horses while its descendant, a Warrior, trundles down to await its turn to launch. Both Pipers have their place and purpose—and price!

Colt's flying characteristics are very much like a Pacer's, only slower. Above 3,000ft the rate of climb deteriorates fairly rapidly; down to less than 400fpm above 5,000ft. Cruise will also be down slightly from its larger horsepower relative—105mph at optimum altitude of 5,000ft.

The Colt may be the best two-seat airplane in the rag-wing market. If you want to go play with older Pipers, this is a good way to spend less than $10,000 to get started.

Colt Rating
Investment: #3
Utility: #4
Popularity: #4

Colt Specifications
Engine: Lycoming O-235-C1, 108hp at 2,600rpm 2,400hr TBO
Maximum Weight: 1,650lb
Fuel Capacity: 36gal
Maximum Speed: 120mph
Cruise 75% Power at Sea Level: 108mph
Fuel Consumption: 5.8gph
Range: 690 miles
Rate of Climb at Sea Level: 610fpm
Service Ceiling: 12,000ft
Stall Speed: 56mph (flaps down)
Standard Empty Weight: 940lb
Maximum Useful Load: 710lb
Wing Span: 29.3ft
Length: 20.2ft
Height: 100in

Chapter 2

The First Little Indians

Cherokee 140 and 150

The Cherokee PA-28, be it 140, 150, or 180hp, was a big step up for Piper. The series was designed to be an all metal airplane with a tricycle landing gear, four seats (rear seats optional on 1964 140s), and a laminar-flow wing, sometimes referred to as a "Hershey-Bar" wing due to its lack of taper and because of its thickness. The Cherokee 150 was introduced in 1962 with a 150hp Lycoming engine and remained in production through 1967. The Cherokee 140 was introduced in 1964 as a trainer model with a 140hp Lycoming engine. In 1965, the Cherokee 140 was fitted with the 150hp engine and gained four seats, wheel pants as standard, and was called the Cruiser. From then on, Cherokee 140s were all fitted with 150hp Lycoming engines.

In 1971, the Flite Liner, a stripped C-140—minus wheel pants and the rear seats—became available to Piper Flite Centers (hence the name "Flite Liner"). Whatever it was called, it now responds to the tower call of plain "Cherokee"; be it 140, 150, or 235hp, Cherokee 140 or Dakota—they're all called the same over the radio.

The most common variety of the smallest Cherokee is the 140, regardless of seats, spats, or power. Most of them now have all four seats on board and numerous other changes added over their 30-year life span.

The 140 is an honest 110mph airplane, 115mph if lightly loaded and if the engine's fairly new. If you watch the weight and bal-

The first little Indian of the Piper Cherokee tribe was the diminutive PA-28-140 Cherokee Cruiser, an entry level airplane that was intended for sport and training applications.

Piper just gushed about their new PA-28-140B back in the early seventies: "Roomy two place seating . . . Dynaflair wheel speed fairings add 3 miles to cruise to 133mph . . . SportsPower console grouping of throttle and mixture controls . . . ample space for full IFR, choice of radios and autopilot." From the Piper copy, you'd think that with a few of these you could start an airline.

ance quite closely, four people can be loaded, smaller bodies in the back, and 2hr of fuel carried. This will give you about a 150-mile range with fuel reserves. Not exactly across-the-country capability, but enough for a weekend trip.

Later models of the 140 gained a throttle quadrant, overhead air vents, standard toe brakes, and air conditioning. The air conditioning brings with it a 70lb weight penalty, so you might be better off to locate an airplane without it or consider having it removed. I've flown a number of 140s, 180s, and Archers with air conditioning—it's nice on the ground on a hot day; not so nice when you only have 450–500lb of useful load after the tanks are filled.

Well, the Cherokee 140 is the first airplane that I owned. After the initial 100hr, I wasn't too sure who owned who, but I think I

was ahead on points. I acquired this little 150hp banger through an FBO at Reid-Hillview Airport near San Jose, California. It turned out to be one of the better deals I ever made. The owner of the FBO and I became

When it was introduced, the Cherokee 140 Cruiser was promoted as a four-seater that cost thousands of dollars less than the competition. As this artist's rendering shows, there are indeed four seats in the Cruiser, but you need to be careful what you put in them. This is not an airplane for taking four beefy adults to the mountains on a hot summer day.

Cherokee 140 and 150 Typical Specifications
Engine: Lycoming O-320-E2A, 150hp, 2,000hr TBO
Maximum Weight: 2,150lb
Fuel Capacity: 36gal (standard), 50gal (optional)
Maximum Speed: 142mph
Cruise Speed: 135mph
Fuel Consumption: 8gph
Range: 720 miles
Rate of Climb at Sea Level: 631fpm
Service Ceiling: 10,950ft
Takeoff over 50ft Obstacle: 1,700ft
Takeoff Ground Run: 800ft
Landing over 50ft Obstacle: 1,090ft
Ground Roll: 535ft
Stall Speed: 55mph (flaps extended)
Standard Empty Weight: 1,274lb
Maximum Useful Load: 676lb
Wing Span: 30ft
Length: 23ft 4in
Height: 7ft 4in

was time for me to own my very own airplane. No more scheduling problems, no more late returns, no more dog hairs all over the seats (really!), no more being able to write squawks down on a time sheet and have them miraculously repaired the next time I jumped in that particular airplane. Also, no more brand-new King or Collins radios. More on that later.

Among Doug Remington, owner of Flying Country Club (FCC), the FBO at Reid-Hillview, and myself we were able to come up with a 1967 Cherokee 140, 1,260hr TT. It had belonged to an elderly gentleman who had decided at age 70 to pack it up, so after a pre-purchase inspection and $10,000 changing hands, it was my very own airplane. I was ready to make my very own mistakes and pay for them out of my very own bank account.

Actually the 140 wasn't a bad airplane to own as a first-time purchase. It's a very forgiving airplane with a top speed slow enough to keep most people honest.

I had a hard time getting accustomed to feeling the ignition key in my pocket. Having that key meant I could go out to the airport anytime, day or night, get in my airplane, and go anywhere I pleased. I even would take my lunch hour and go for a short hop. Sometimes

fast friends and this book would not have been written without his more-than-generous help.

I had been renting nice, shiny new Archers, Warriors, and Arrows for the past two years at another FBO that had a very large fleet of tax-writeoff-new Pipers, but I was getting tired of all the problems inherent with renting. Like a lot of people, I figured it

This little formation flight shows the external differences between the Cherokee 140 Cruiser and the Cherokee Flite Liner—spats for the gear, an option that Piper was pushing, and a fairing for the fin were not carried over to the Flite Liner. Inside, besides the additional power in the Flite Liner's engine, both models now had redesigned steering and braking systems, with toe brakes finally standard in 1973.

The little Cherokee 140 Cruiser was introduced in 1961 and stayed in production until 1974, when the Warrior was introduced. It dominated its segment of the market for many years. The 140 chugs along behind a 150hp Lycoming with 2,000hr TBO. While Piper claimed a 133mph cruise, few airframes available today will produce that.

The PA-28 Cherokee 140 panel. Despite what the factory said about the panel, there isn't enough room here for all the radios and nav systems you might want to install. It is a cozy little place, with room for the basics.

a little more than lunch hour went by. Strange feeling to be paged in an airplane 40 miles away from the radio in the truck and be able to answer the call within 20min. I was once on call in San Jose while spending a nice evening in a casino at Lake Tahoe, 1 hr away by plane. Of course the pager had to go off as the main course was being served. I excused myself, made a long-distance phone call to the client, and determined that my presence was required back in Silicon Valley at a computer chip company 15 miles north of San Jose.

I returned to my guests (one who flew up with me and two who lived at the lake), and explained the situation. I told them I would catch up to them later. A quick preflight and I was off to San Jose. My company had a 2hr response time from the initial call, so the power stayed at full throttle all the way back. I landed, tied down, and grabbed the service truck so fast that I was still flying the airplane as the truck hit the freeway.

I don't remember much about the particular problem, just that it was easily repaired

This little Indian has 150hp and was, in its day during the seventies, an extremely popular trainer when Piper was calling it the Flite Liner. Over sixty paint schemes were offered, all of which are now likely to be well-oxidized.

Back in 1971 Piper, along with the competition, was selling the idea that Mom and the kids could fly, too, and that the Piper engineers had even thoughtfully provided plenty of extra headroom to accommodate the hairdos of the era.

"We call this thing a 'flap,' m'am," the gent seems to be saying while trying to introduce a prospective student to a Flite Liner.

and I was at the client's building in less than 45min. He asked me where I had come from, was I on another call when his came in. There are certain times when a camera would be useful and this was one of them. When I told him I came down from Lake Tahoe and planned on being back there in one-and-a-half hours, his face showed that he thought my company employed madmen and pathological liars. He was quite amazed when I explained the airplane game to him, and said,

"If you can cover ground that fast, maybe I should see about lessons." On that note, I left, saying even though I missed the main course, I might be able to get back in time for desert. With that kind of a start, the weekend could go nowhere but up. It was one time I really didn't mind being on call.

The Cherokee 140 has 50gal tanks, 10gal more than its nearest competitor, the Cessna 172. At a 8gph fuel burn and a 100kt cruising speed, that makes for another hour plus travel over the 172. In the western US, sometimes the range is needed. I took the 140 down into Baja, California, a number of times and if I would have taken a 172 instead, I'd probably have ended up paddling the last 50 miles or so.

Nothing is perfect, not even my first airplane. One of its favorite quirks was not wanting to start on a cold morning. The battery lived in an aft compartment and was connected to the engine with a too-small-gauge cable. On more than a few cold mornings on cross-country I had to get the airport start-cart to give the battery a little kick. The engine would always start on the second revolution, but on a cold morning it only turned over once. A light taste of the jumper and usually ten dollars—we were on our way. I finally got tired of being stranded or having to wait till the sun came up, so I bought 15ft of copper

From 1972 onward, air conditioning was an option on Cherokees. The condenser system extended from the belly of the beast during cruise; it retracted if full throttle was applied.

Here's a wider view of the air conditioning condenser in the extended position. Piper carefully avoided mentioning in its ads for the system just how much performance deteriorated with the condenser out there, acting like a speed brake—knocking about 10kt off cruise.

arc-welding cable and replaced the existing line, connectors and all. Presto—no more starting problems.

One other problem that was a little more serious was the old radios and their worn out plugs. I had two Narco MK-12 tube-type radios in the panel that gave more trouble than did all the rest of the airplane, together. There is a transmit relay in the radio that goes intermittent when it gets old. Also the connector between the radio and the amplifier gets corroded, cutting off the power.

Now if you had to guess where both of the radios failed simultaneously and knew my name is Murphy, where would you think? Well, close, but it was actually 10 miles out of home base on a Special VFR approach. (One mile visibility and clear of clouds, kind of a VFR-IFR approach some think is not a good way to land.) One radio had gone to sleep but the other was still talking to me, so on we pressed.

Right after the tower called me—"79 Kilo, 5 miles from airport, stay outside airport traffic area and remain VFR until cleared to enter"—the last radio decided to join its brother in quiet repose. I was anything but reposed. Here I was flying 360s, 5 miles out from an airport, waiting for the last guy to land and clear the active so I could follow and get down where the ground was visible, when both my radios went away. Another pilot was riding in the copilot's seat watching me go through all this. His only comment: "Is it always this much fun flying with you?"

I told him to reach under the right side of the panel where he would find two white connectors about 3in wide. "Grab one and pull it about one-half inch apart, then push it back together firmly," I said. "Which one?," he asked while reaching past the yoke to find the junctions. "I don't care which one, I'll take any radio!" was my answer. He had been through old airplane ownership before and had an idea of what to do. After some twisting and pulling, the number two radio came to life. I caught the last two syllables of a transmission from the tower. I keyed the mike, "Reid tower, was the last transmission for 79 Kilo?"

"79 Kilo, Reid Tower, did you read my last transmission?"

The controls for the cabin heat/air conditioning normally were on the far right side of the panel.

"Tower, negative on the last, I've been having radio problems, corrected now."

"79 Kilo, ok, cleared to land Runway 31. Do you wish to over-fly the airfield and make an overhead approach?"

"Roger, Tower, 79 Kilo will over-fly the runway and approach from overhead."

Tower: "79 Kilo, affirmative, call overhead runway."

After we flew into the ATA and descended another 1,000ft, the ground became visible. Another 2min and the runway appeared off to the right.

"Reid Tower, Cherokee 79 Kilo, overhead Runway 31 for landing."

"79 Kilo, cleared to land Runway 31 Right, lights are on."

"Tower, 79 Kilo, many thanks."

After that little vignette, I figured a new radio would go a long way towards saving what little was left of my sanity. A trip to my local radio shop showed that a new King KX-155 would cost roughly one third the value of the airplane to have installed, so I went looking for other ideas. Turns out there's something called "yellow tag." If an item of avionics has been yellow-tagged, then it is fit to go back into service. Not everything in it has been rebuilt, just what is necessary. Everything else is checked out for proper function prior to sale.

I was able to find a good King KX-170 B Nav/Com for under $1,000 installed, and it was the first $1,000 I was glad to part with. What a difference. I blew another wad of money on an intercom under the theory that it would be cheaper to install while the radio was out. Then the woman in my life took pity on me and bought me a set of David Clark H10-30 headsets for my future birthday. Wow, did the world ever open up. Why, I could talk to people and hear what they say. This new stuff is all right.

The moral to the story, if there needs to be one, is: After the airplane's running gear is all ok, make sure that your radios are the best you can afford. In the last couple of years, I've taken to carrying a hand-held radio in my flight bag; it's cheap insurance and peace of mind. My Terra TPX 720 hand-held is somewhat dated and a bit bulky, but it always works and that's what counts. I can plug my headset and push-to-talk switch into the Terra and have 2–3hr of radio. Like most others, it can be plugged into a cigarette lighter if the airplane is so equipped. Or a charging jack can be installed under the panel at a very nominal cost.

Besides old avionics, a couple of other problem areas are particular to the Cherokee 140, 150, 160, 180, and 235 series. On pre-1967 Cherokees, leaking fuel tanks can be a real pain. The only fail-safe way to ensure fuel doesn't leak on your new shoes is to pull the tanks and have them re-sealed. Not quite a simple job. It's rather expensive, but if done right, should not reoccur during your ownership of the airplane.

Another particular soft spot on the Cherokee 140 through 180 are the 7/16in exhaust valves fitted to the Lycoming O-320. If they are still there at this late date, which is quite unlikely, then the engine TBO is 1,200hr. There's an AD requiring a 500hr check if the smaller valves are still present. Seeing as how almost all of the Cherokee 140 at 150 engines are on their second or third (or more) rebuild, this should not be a problem.

The Cherokee 150 is virtually the same airplane as the Cherokee 140. Both have the same engine, horsepower, top speed, gross load, fuel capacity, and so on. The 140 was originally intended to be a two-seat trainer, but almost all of them were converted to four seats at a later date. Piper finally figured out that they were building two airplanes whose only difference was a hat shelf and a model designation. The 150 was discontinued in 1967.

Cherokee 160

The Cherokee 160 was introduced in 1962 as a slightly more powerful version of the 140/150 series—same engine, 10hp more and a 100lb higher useful load. If you're trying to stay low dollar, this is an airplane that can be loaded with four people with about a 2hr flight range and still stay within weight and balance. Its 50gal fuel load weighs 300lb, leaving 690lb as load that can be carried in the seats. If you drop the fuel load to 30gal, that adds another 120lb for passengers giving a total of 810lb in the cabin. That's 202.5lb per seat with enough fuel to go 2.2hr with 10gal reserve.

If two of the passengers are smaller, then you can carry more fuel on board for a longer trip. Don't expect a Cherokee 160 to leap off the runway when it is full of fuel and people, but it will lift off in 775ft of ground roll if you do your part.

All the bad habits of the early Cherokee 140s are carried over to the 160—and there weren't many. Its useful load goes up 50lb

This view of a 1972 vintage panel has the "climate control center" on the far right. Starting that year, too, Piper added a cover for the breaker panel, shown here on the extreme lower right.

Cherokee 160 Rating
Investment: #3
Utility: #3
Popularity: #3

over the Cherokee 150, plus there's a very slight gain in cruising speed, but you'd be hard pressed to notice the difference. Last built in 1967, a good one can be had for around $20,000, and it probably will still be worth $20,000 five years from now.

Cherokee 180

Installing a 180hp Lycoming on the basic Cherokee airframe in 1963 made it a true four-place airplane, and it has become one of the most popular airplanes ever built. Cherokee 180s were built until 1975.

The 180 is the low-wing equivalent of a Cessna 172. The extra 20hp gives the Piper a 10kt cruise speed advantage and a higher payload advantage over the 172. Having a 50gal tank instead of the Skyhawk's standard 40gal tank gives the range advantage to the Cherokee 180. If the Skyhawk has the larger 62gal tanks, it can beat the Cherokee 180 in range, but the tradeoff is that someone will have to ride the bus. The Cherokee 180's useful load after filling the tanks is 875lb. Subtract another 100lb for a real-life airplane with avionics and other equipment for a real world load of 775lb with gas for a 4hr flight time at 140mph, or 560 miles.

In real travel, this allows you to take four people, baggage, and a full fuel load nonstop from San Jose, California, to Portland, Oregon, if the winds are right. Many's the time I took a Cherokee 180 or its bigger brother, the Archer, for a nonstop run from San Jose to Mexicali on the Cal-Mex border below Imperial County, as a first stop on a trip to Puerto Vallarta, Manzanillo, or other points south on the Mexican coast. The difference in performance between the "Hershey-Bar" winged Cherokee 180 and the Archer with its long-taper wing isn't worth consideration. Mostly what you gain from the Archer is a different look from the "old-fashioned" wing of any Cherokee 180 built before 1976. If the older short-wing Cherokee 180 looks as good to you as the Archer, then go look for a good used Cherokee 180. Archers are currently smoking through the stratosphere in value, while a good medium time 180 can be found for thousands less.

The Cherokee 235 was intended to be a serious, working airplane in its class: space for four and power to get them up and around. A 235hp Lycoming engine with 1,500hr TBO gave the aircraft a rated 1,433lb of useful load, a top speed of 169mph, and a cruise of 159mph (75 percent power at 7,000ft).

Why, I know of a clean 1963 Cherokee 180 with only 1,700hr TT and 1,000hr since top end rebuild (STOP), fully IFR, and new Archer-pattern paint that can be had for under $24,000. It's up in northern California, but you should be able to find a corrosion-free, low-time Cherokee 180 at one of your nearby airports. Go get one of the club rentals for a weekend and play airport bum. You'd be surprised at what comes out of hangars on Saturday and Sunday. A lot of deals are made without anything appearing in an ad. At the least, you will meet some interesting people, and you might learn a little in the process.

Cherokee and Pathfinder 235

The Cherokee 235 and Pathfinder (235 from now on) compares closely to the Cessna 182 in gross weight and performance. Piper first introduced the 235 in 1964 as a load-hauling fixed-gear single. They were built until 1978.

The 235 has a cruise speed up with a number of retractable singles, but the gear is down and welded, which makes it easier to fly and less of a risk to your insurance carrier. With the optional tanks, the 235 can carry 84gal of fuel, which weighs 504lb. When subtracted from the useful load of 1,465lb, you're left with 961lb of people and cargo capability. Figure another 100lb of load lost to avionics, leaving 861lb to play with. *Flying* magazine says in its April 1993 issue that the 235 ". . . can carry about everything that will fit into the door."

The only transition a Cherokee 140 pilot would have to make to a 235 is from a fixed-pitch propeller to a constant-speed version. Oh yeah, you would also have to become familiar with the difference in performance between a lightly loaded Cherokee 140 and a 235. The 140 will climb out at 600fpm under normal conditions, whereas a 235 will go up-

With that extra power the Cherokee 235 has pretty good short-field performance: a 600ft takeoff run was claimed by Piper. With the tanks topped off at 84gal, a range of over 1,100 miles was specified by the builder. Two hundred pounds of baggage could be carried in the compartment behind the cabin.

Cherokee 235 Typical Specifications
Engine: Lycoming O-540-B4B5, 235hp, 2,000hr TBO
Maximum Weight: 2,900lb
Fuel Capacity: 50gal, (standard), 84gal (optional)
Maximum Speed: 161mph
Cruise Speed: 153mph
Fuel Consumption: 12.5gph
Range 75% Power at 7,000ft: 915 miles
Rate of Climb at Sea Level: 825fpm
Service Ceiling: 14,500ft
Takeoff over 50ft Obstacle: 1,040ft
Takeoff Ground Run: 600ft
Landing over 50ft Obstacle: 1,060ft
Ground Roll: 550ft
Stall Speed: 60mph
Standard Empty Weight: 1,435lb
Maximum Useful Load: 1,465lb
Wing Span: 32ft
Length: 23ft 8in (stretched to 24ft 1 in, with larger tail, in 1973)
Height: 7ft 3in (changed to 7ft 6in in 1973)

stairs at over 1,100fpm with one person on board and a light load of fuel. The Cherokee 235's short-field performance is also rather impressive. With a 10kt headwind, a good pilot can get a lightly loaded 235 off in less than 500ft. The book says 600ft, but that's for an airplane at gross weight with no headwind.

If your requirements are for a four-place airplane that will haul a large load for 600 miles or more, and you want the simplicity of fixed gear, then the Cherokee 235 is your airplane. It's a lot of other people's airplane, too. And they know what it's worth. Come prepared to spend some money to get a good one. The nice part is that the 235 has always been in demand and has had high resale value, so 235s are generally well maintained. The market indicates that what few 235s are for sale are in excellent condition. A 1964, with 2,250hr TT and a runout engine, is going for $29,000. A 1973, loaded, is going for

This 1972 factory photograph promoted the 235 as an entry level business aircraft, although with four beefy gents aboard—with baggage—the 235's short-field performance was likely to be substantially degraded.

The Cherokee 235 really was, and still is, a practical airplane that could go places and do things. The rear seats come out without tools; payload, range and speed are all up into the practical range, and there are enough of them around to choose from. The 235 grew up to become the Dakota. Transition from an entry level airplane like the 140 is short and sweet; the main skill you need to learn is to manage a constant-speed prop. The 235 was originally christened the Pathfinder by Piper marketing, but the name quickly disappeared and it is now just called the 235 after its horsepower rating.

$56,000. One thing seems to run through all the Cherokee 235s for sale: low-time. Most of these 25–30-year-old airplanes are running around with less than 2,500hr TT. None of them were used as a trainer. This might be the airplane you buy as an investment, and own as a keeper.

This approximately quarter-century-old airframe remains in airworthy condition and is here accelerating through about 50kt IAS. These planes are still popular and desirable, despite their age, and can probably be sold for their purchase price if reasonably maintained. We don't know if Piper actually had a department responsible for coming up with odd and imaginative names for what was essentially the same basic airplane, but Charger was one name briefly applied to the PA-28-235—also known as the Pathfinder.

Despite the close resemblance to its weak little brother, the 235 is a muscular, agile airplane: under real-world conditions you can easily get it off with a 500ft takeoff run, climb out at 1100fpm, and not come back to earth for 600 miles. Even thirty years after rolling out the factory door these airplanes are holding their value and earning their keep.

Chapter 3

The Newer Little Indians

Warrior and Archer

The Warrior is a direct descendant of the Cherokee 140, first seen in the mid-1960s. Originally fitted with the same 150hp engine as the 140, the Warrior was only offered for one year, 1974. In 1975 Piper upped the horsepower to 160 and changed the name to the Warrior II where it stays today. The Cherokee 140 had a straight "Hershey-Bar" wing, but when the Warrior II made its debut, it arrived with a new tapered-wing design that was not only more efficient, with increased control power and crisper control, but also gave Piper something to tout in their advertising.

In 1978, Piper cleaned up the airframe and installed landing gear strut fairings for a

"All new for 1974," says the Piper ad copy, "the Piper Warrior, the first of the next generation of 4-place family aircraft, gains maximum performance from revolutionary tapered wing." The PA-28 Cherokee Warrior is a slightly improved Cherokee 150 with a bit more wing, a bit more fuel, and a little more payload—an incremental improvement. A total of 703 were built in 1974, the first year of production.

A 1976 vintage Warrior II shows its Cherokee ancestry. The little four-place assumed primary flight training duties for the Piper stable with the demise of the Tomahawk line and is used far more frequently as a trainer than its designers probably intended. It's got a 160hp Lycoming under the cowling with 2,000hr TBO, carries 50gal of fuel, and is grossed out at 2,325lb.

7kt published increase in cruise speed. Other than a new prop spinner and a change to a velour interior, that's about all the improvements it's seen.

Some who have flown the Cherokee 140 and the Warrior back to back, say that there isn't a great deal of difference between the two, but I've owned one and flown the other for over 300hr, and I think the difference is quite noticeable. The Warrior feels much crisper and its roll rate is higher than the 140's. Of course I'd never try to see what kind of response you'd see in an aileron roll or anything of the kind; however, what playing around I've done over the ocean seems to show that the new wing works well for control with less work at the yoke. Because of the increased roll response, the pilot can handle crosswind landings more comfortably, leaving fewer black lines and squealing noises on landings.

With the demise of the Tomahawk in 1982 and the Super Cub in 1992, the Warrior II was now Piper's entry level airplane. In the

The Warrior IIs were built from 1975 on and featured the tapered wing that Piper claimed made a major improvement in handling. Most earlier Warriors, along with Cherokees, have the straight "Hershey-Bar" wing.

past, the Warrior has been used as a primary trainer for those pilots who wanted to fly a low-wing single and liked the looks and performance of Piper's airplanes. A total of 4,052 Warriors and Warrior IIs were built from 1974 to 1986 with, perhaps, another 100 Warrior IIs and a slightly smaller number of stripped down, two-seat Warrior IIs, called Cadets, sold from 1989 to 1991. The Cadet was intended to be a low-cost VFR trainer, sold only to flight schools. At a base price of $59,995 in 1990, compared to the Warrior II's $88,900, Piper lost money on every one they made.

Anyone who is at least a mediocre pilot (me) can get a Warrior in to a 2,000ft landing strip without any problem. The factory guys could do it with slightly less than a 600ft ground roll, but for those of us with older engines, eyes, and responses, somewhere in the 900ft realm is much more like it. There's a restaurant halfway down Interstate 5 in California called Harris Ranch Restaurant. Its big claim to fame is the best fillet mignon west of Pahrump (that's in Nevada). Its other major advantage is in having a runway right on the property, along Interstate 5. The only, ever so slight, minor, little problem is that the runway is 2,800ft in length and 30ft wide.

Now this wouldn't be so bad if the wind didn't blow from time to time, or if the overpass from I-5 to Highway 198 wasn't directly in line with Runway 32, or that the field

didn't look to be about the width of a pencil lead when seen along the freeway while on final. All this for a new pilot (me, again) making his first approach with a planeload of not-so-crazy-about-flying passengers who had heard about the above mentioned charcoaled-cow and were willing to share the one-hour flight there from San Jose International (SJC) with me. They were enjoying the ride. I, on the other hand, was watching the wind sock shift back and forth across the runway in the fading light as darkness crept up on us. I had left SJC late so as to arrive at Harris Ranch in time to enjoy a twilight dinner. Now I was enjoying the thought of making a crosswind landing on a narrow strip that I had never been into before. Lucky for me, darkness was soon to come along; kind of helped me make up my mind about landing soon. I'd like to say that my thoughts at the time were centered on that first bite of steak, but those of you who have been in like situations would

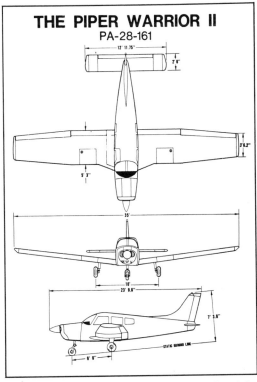

THE PIPER WARRIOR II
PA-28-161

This piper three-view drawing shows details of the Warrior II's new wing.

Warrior II Typical Specifications
Engine: Lycoming O-320-D3D, 160hp, 2,000hr TBO
Maximum Weight: 2,325lb
Fuel Capacity: 50gal
Maximum Speed at Sea Level: 126kt
Maximum Cruise: 121kt
Range: 520nm
Rate of Climb at Sea Level: 710fpm
Service Ceiling: 14,000ft
Takeoff Ground Run: 975ft
Takeoff Over 50ft Obstacle: 1,490ft
Landing Ground Roll: 595ft
Landing Over 50ft Obstacle: 1,115ft
Stall Speed: 43kt (flaps extended); 48kt (flaps up)
Standard Empty Weight: 1,344lb
Maximum Useful Load: 981lb
Wing Span: 35ft
Length: 23.8ft
Height: 7.3ft

Archer and Archer II Typical Specifications
Engine: Lycoming O-360-A4M, 180hp, 2,000hr TBO
Maximum Weight: 2,550lb
Fuel Capacity: 50gal
Maximum Speed: 129kt
Cruise Speed: 129kt
Range: 590–670nm
Rate of Climb at Sea Level: 740fpm
Service Ceiling: 13,650ft
Takeoff Ground Run: 870ft
Takeoff over 50ft Obstacle: 1,625ft
Landing Ground Roll: 925ft
Landing over 50ft Obstacle: 1,390ft
Stall Speed: 53kt (flaps extended); 59kt (flaps up)
Standard Empty Weight: 1,414lb
Maximum Useful Load: 1,136lb
Wing Span: 35ft
Length: 23.8ft
Height: 7.3ft

Some of the earlier Warrior Is had the tapered wing; this is a 1973 model the factory was using to promote the new design. Piper said of the new design, "The new wing with its distinctive 100-inch long ailerons and leading edge reflex gives the Warrior increased control power without increasing roll control forces. The result is faster roll response. Crosswind landings are more comfortable and the pilots have excellent roll control throughout stall." The author concurs, but other pilots don't notice the difference.

probably not believe me. One nice thing, the last couple of flights in the Warrior II had been check-outs for transition from a Cessna 172 and I had spent a lot of time that I considered wasted practicing short-field landings. Yes, I did thank my instructor when I saw her again the next week. I wouldn't try to palm off the landing totally on my sterling abilities, though. A lot of the credit had to go to the Piper and the ability of the Warrior wing to

The Warrior II was, and is, an honest four-place airplane that could—like its forebearers in the Cherokee clan, the 180 and 235—earn its keep. Maximum useful load is 981lb, range is up to 560nm, and maximum cruise is up to 127kt (75 percent power at 9,000ft).

let me get it on the ground without more than one or two tense moments. The food was great too!

The takeoff after the sun had set and the wind died down was no problem, but I admit to thinking about it a little bit during dinner. It was a nice clear flight home with the lights of San Jose visible from 50 miles out. Now that I've been flying for a few more years, the landings aren't quite so hard as during my first 100hr, but I still don't like 30ft wide runways and crosswinds any better than I did fifteen years ago.

The Piper Archer is the Warrior with 20hp more and, depending on equipment, about 150lb more payload. The Archer was only around during 1975, being superseded by the tapered-wing Archer II in 1976. The book says to expect to see 129kt flat out, about 4kt less than a similarly equipped Cessna Hawk XP. All the Archers that I've flown

must have had smaller horses or something because I don't think I have ever seen more than 120kt true airspeed on any of them. Not that the book is incorrect, but every little bit helps, especially when it comes to speed from an airplane. After all, one of the reasons you buy an airplane is to go fast—speed sells. Quite possibly someone did get an Archer II to go a measured 129kt, but most of us don't fly with the throttle pushed to the engine cases and 11gal of fuel in the tanks at 500ft AGL. Most manufacturers get their airplanes to show a set of numbers on the airspeed indicator (ASI) that you and I would have a hard time duplicating with the spinner horizontal. I mean, I owned a 1979 Mooney 201 for a few years and I was never able to get it to go 201mph.

Were I in the Warrior or Archer market today, what would I look for? Well, with most of the general aviation fleet getting along in

The Lycoming O-320-D3D is a 160hp engine with a 2,000hr TBO that will push the Warrior II along at a maximum 126kt (2,700rpm at sea level) and will climb out at 710fpm and will take it up to a 14,000ft service ceiling.

This little Warrior is all wound up and is about to taxi off to battle, but that front strut looks kind of low—a chronic problem and something to check for when shopping for an airframe. There ought to be about another 2in of strut showing. Time to check and probably replace the seals on that front strut, and recharge with nitrogen.

age, condition and total time are more important than the particular year of the airplane. If the Warrior has 4,000–6,000hr on it and it's less than twelve years old, chances are that it acquired most of those hours flying sweaty-palmed students around the pattern while they suffered with the intricacies of powered flight for the first time. Not that buying a former trainer airplane from a flight school would be a bad idea as the airplane will have been maintained quite well. After all, it's the tool they use to make money. If it don't fly, the dollars don't arrive, so the flight school will be more motivated to keep it flying in good shape. If you figure that most general aviation airframes are good for 20,000hr before they wear out, then a Warrior with 4,500hr and a low-time engine would have a long way to go before it is turned in at the recycle plant.

When you've found that particular Warrior or Archer that you just can't wait to throw money at to own, a few things need to

The PA-28-181 Archer II got a 3ft longer wing when it was introduced in 1976, up to 35ft, adding 100lb to the useful load.

be covered before money changes hands. I know you've heard me say it before, but remember, the first thing that gets inspected is the paperwork, the logbooks. If the logs are gone, find another airplane to buy. No paper trail, no airplane sale.

Neither the Archer nor the Warrior really have any major bad habits. Piper pretty much figured it out on the Cherokee 140–180 series and didn't build in many problems. Like its bigger relation, the Dakota, the Archer and the Warrior are a gentle, forgiving airplane to fly and respond well to a light touch on the controls. If you are flying one as a student pilot and don't believe that the airplane does anything without copious amounts of sweat and muscle, remember, it does get easier. If you still aren't convinced, go buy an hour in the front seat of a Citabria and then come back to the Warrior. You'll see.

Given the opportunity, I wouldn't hesitate a minute to own another Archer. With fuel to the indicator tabs in the tanks, it will carry four people from San Jose International (56ft MSL) to South Lake Tahoe Airport (6,264ft MSL) for an evening's dinner at one of the state-line casinos and be quite willing to make the one-hour-and-some flight back home at midnight. Keeping in mind that density altitude can easily turn a airplane into a fast car with wings, one wants to plan the trip carefully. A 90deg outside air temperature (OAT) at Tahoe will make the airplane think it's at 9,500ft. The rate of climb for anything under 235hp is rather low at that altitude and the rocks a few miles from the end of Runway 18 are a real impediment to travel. Going the other way puts you out over the lake, a nice view if you are interested, but not when the airplane is laboring to grab the next 50ft of altitude.

More than once we've played racetrack down the lake while trying to get up to a safe level to cross Echo Summit at 10,000ft AGL or better for a safe ride over the Sierra Nevadas. Flying around Lake Tahoe while waiting for the altimeter to wind up is a nice way to look at the view; however, on a hot day climbing 3,500ft with a high density altitude is not the best way to use an airplane. I will say that the view out the plexiglass while flying over the Sierra Nevadas on a moonlit night with the

visibility 76–80 miles has to be one of the high points of my life.

When the snow is still dusting the peaks and the moon is straight overhead, the air is still, the ride is smooth and it's almost better than daylight. I can see the beacon at Placerville Airport (Hangtown VOR, HNW 115.5; if nothing else, the old 49ers came up with colorful names for their towns) as soon as the nose crests the mountaintops. It's only 38 miles southwest from South Lake Tahoe Airport, so there's about a 10min period of time when things could get a little tense, unless one was good at landing uphill on rocks if the windmill quits. I've made the trip for over eleven years now, but I will admit to doing a real good preflight on the Archer before I go fly over the granite.

I could go through the usual sayings about the controls falling easily to hand and a few more overworked similes about airplanes. As every pilot knows, though, the

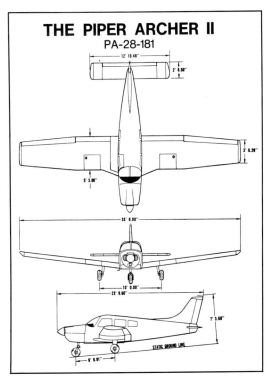

THE PIPER ARCHER II
PA-28-181

The dimensions of the Archer II are suspiciously like those of its older brothers, the Cherokee and Warrior lines.

The Piper Archer II was powered by a 180hp Lycoming 0-360 engine. The Lycoming 0-360 is one of the great aircraft engines of all time and gives the Archer a 740fpm climb.

The Archer II cruises at 144mph, has a range of 770 miles (75 percent power), and a service ceiling of almost 14,000ft; fuel consumption is as low as 8.8gph. By the early 1980s, when this picture was made, men were still wearing bell-bottom suit pants but the Piper Archer had matured into a pretty modern single. Although the lines are the same, the Archer has 20hp over the Warrior and will carry another 150lb aloft. It has carried the author all over the western United States and most of Mexico.

only way that any airplane will feel comfortable to fly is to go spend lots of hours behind the yoke, preferably while flying. The Archer is a logical move up from the Warrior for a novice pilot. If all your preliminary flight training has been taken in the Warrior, then there really is nothing new to learn about the bigger-engined Archer.

The O-360-A4M Lycoming engine in the nose of the Archer is considered, along with its smaller brother the O-320 in the Warrior, to be one of the most reliable engines available in an airplane. With a modicum of care and maintenance, the O-360-A4M will easily put out its rated power for the full 2,000hr TBO. The O (opposed) -360 (cubic inch) -A4M (model designation) engine is rated at 180hp at sea level, but very seldom does it run at full power. Only at takeoff from an airport with an elevation very close to sea level will the 180hp be available for operation. Most pilots pull back the power 5min after takeoff, or when the airplane reaches a safe altitude, until the tachometer drops 200–400rpm.

Once at cruising altitude, the throttle is set to produce a rated percentage of the 180hp, usually in the 65–75 percent range. If the Archer is going to be flown at a high altitude of 8,000–11,000ft for an extended cross country over high terrain, even full throttle the engine will only produce about 67 percent of its rated power. As the airplane climbs into thinner air, the engine cannot get enough oxygen to make rated horsepower. If it wasn't for the ability of the mixture control to lean out the amount of fuel going to the engine, operation in the higher altitudes would be almost impossible. The engine would be ingesting much more gasoline than it could mix with the available oxygen at altitude, causing the engine to smoke, run rough, and in some cases quit operating.

Talking to a few flight schools operating Warriors and Archers, I found that, unless some part failed or the airplane was operated without fuel in the tanks, all the airplanes went to TBO without major problems. Some private individuals have been known to operate an engine 200–300hr over TBO without problems, a practice neither Lycoming nor I recommend. Some say that if you take oil samples for analysis every 50hr, watch oil

The extra wing span really shows on this shot. Besides adding to payload, the additional 3ft makes a big difference in roll response.

Here's a 1973 Cherokee 235, the forerunner to the Dakota, called the Pathfinder by Piper when this shot was made. It shows 235hp struggling with four fat folks aboard on a high, hot day to gain altitude before turning east across those mountains in the background. But at least they are traveling in style; Piper redesigned the windows on the Cherokee in 1973 for what it called a "sleeker look" on the 180hp and 235hp versions of the beast.

consumption and look for any unusual change in the operating characteristics of the engine, there is no reason that a motor can't be operated past TBO. I prefer to know that all the parts in the engine were rebuilt when the manufacturer specified. I feel much safer in an airplane that hasn't reached TBO and the last engine was a factory REMAN. Granted, not all of us can afford to install the best money can buy, but you will feel mighty foolish thinking about how much money you saved on the engine that just stopped in mid-flight.

Dakota and Turbo Dakota

The Dakota is the Cherokee 235 with the Warrior tapered wing and a larger fuel capacity. It has a 1,400lb useful load before fuel. As long as the tires aren't flat after filling the cabin, the Dakota will carry anything that will fit through the door. The standard Dakota is powered by the Lycoming 235hp O-540-J3A5D with a 2,000hr TBO, while the Turbo has a Continental 200hp TSIO-360-FB that

---

Dakota and Turbo Dakota Rating
Investment: #1
Utility: #2
Popularity: #1

Dakota and Turbo Dakota Typical Specifications
Engine: Lycoming O-540-J3A5D, 235hp, 2,000hr TBO; Continental TSIO-360-FB, 200hp, 1,800hr TBO (Turbo)
Maximum Weight: 3,000lb; 2,900lb (Turbo)
Fuel Capacity: 77gal
Maximum Speed at Sea Level: 148kt; 143kt (Turbo)
Maximum Cruise: 144kt at 75% power at 9,000ft; 156kt at 75% power at 18,800ft (Turbo)
Range: 696–810nm; 618–647nm (Turbo)
Rate of Climb at Sea Level: 1,110fpm; 902fpm (Turbo)
Service Ceiling: 17,500ft; 20,000ft (Turbo)
Takeoff Ground Run: 886ft; 963ft (Turbo)
Takeoff Over 50ft Obstacle: 1,216ft; 1,402ft (Turbo)
Landing Ground Roll: 640ft; 861ft (Turbo)
Landing Over 50ft Obstacle: 1,530ft; 1,697ft (Turbo)
Stall Speed: 59kt (flaps down); 67kt (flaps up)
Standard Empty Weight: 1,608lb; 1,563lb (Turbo)
Maximum Useful Load: 1,392lb; 1,337lb (Turbo)
Wing Span: 35ft
Length: 25ft
Height: 7.6ft

The Dakota turns the basic Piper low-wing into a four-place workhorse with more useful load than anything else in its class. It was released in two versions at about the same time, a normally-aspirated 235hp Dakota that starts wheezing at about 10,000ft, and the Turbo with 200hp that will stay with you for another few thousand feet. Shown is a 1980 Turbo Dakota.

This Dakota, like the rest, is equipped with an autopilot and a panel stuffed with a wide assortment of expensive systems that help the pilot use the aircraft's speed and range efficiently. As a result, the Dakota is pricey. At the time this was written, 1980 Turbos like this were selling for around $75,000 while 1976 Warriors were going for about half that; Archers go anywhere from $80,000 to $140,000.

One of the first things you'll check out when inspecting a potential purchase is the panel and its contents. This Dakota, sitting in the Lafferty Aircraft Sales hangar in San Jose, California, had one of the old, standard KX 170 radios replaced with an MX 170—a pullout with ten-channel memory, a $500–$1,000 upgrade. Newer aircraft will have a KX 155 installed.

needs to come apart every 1,800hr. A total of 2,800 were built up to 1986; however, as of November 1993, Piper will screw one together for you if you offer them money—probably $215,000 would do!

Cruise speed is in the 144kt range, 156kt for the Turbo version above 18,000ft. It will cover over 800nm still leaving full IFR reserves. If you need to haul a load over high terrain, the Dakota Turbo will do the job, covering 610nm at 18,000ft altitude. Where the high parts of the countryside aren't above 4,500ft, the Dakota really shines. It's an airplane that can carry four real-sized people with their luggage, in air conditioned splendor for four and one-half hours nonstop.

Actual model changes during the production run amounted to a different interior after 1980. Nothing else changed on the airplane. The biggest change on the Turbo for 1980 was that it wasn't there anymore. It was the wrong combination of engine and airframe, going head to head with the Arrow—a faster airplane powered with the same engine.

Both models of the Dakota are doing real well in the resale market. Any one will fetch 80 percent of their new price. Archers and Warriors are moving up so fast that any price stated today will probably be obsolete by tomorrow. The Blue Book shows a 1979 Turbo worth $42,000. The standard Dakota for the same year is actually worth more than $60,000. Real life airplanes, in good condition, are bringing up to a $10,000 premium over book. This goes for the later models as well. A 1991 Dakota will run exactly what it cost new—$173,000—if you can find one. . .they're really scarce. All three airplanes are excellent value for the money.

Here's another Dakota panel in a Lafferty aircraft. This one has just the basic Piper collection of bells and whistles: older King ADF, transponder, a pair of KX 170Bs, VOR indicators, standard King enunciator panel, Piper AutoControl II autopilot. Neither this nor the previous Dakota panel shows lorans, the absence of which is unusual in the Dakota because most of them do a lot of IFR flying.

This Dakota shows one of the many paint schemes you'll find on Piper aircraft. *Lafferty Aircraft Sales*

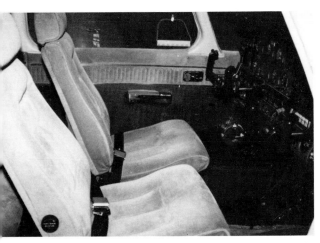

Although the basic airframe concept is essentially the same as the old Cruisers, the interior comfort level of Piper singles has increased almost as fast as their cost. Pilot and second officer seats are fully adjustable, plush, and available in almost any fabric your interior decorator could ask for. *Lafferty Aircraft Sales*

The back-seat passengers haven't done too badly, either. Long gone is the stiff, skimpy little bench seat for those traveling in tourist class. The Dakota's plush high-back seats could use arm rests, but are otherwise quite tolerable for the duration of most flights this aircraft is likely to perform. *Lafferty Aircraft Sales*

Another of the many paint schemes Dakotas have worn over the years. *Lafferty Aircraft Sales*

Chapter 4

The Faster Members of the Tribe

Commanche

The PA-24 Comanche 180 was Piper's smallest entry into the retractable, high speed, single-engine category. First produced in 1958 along with its more-muscular sibling, the Comanche 250, it was a four-place retractable that would cruise at a respectable 160mph—a lot of performance for 180hp. I didn't really think that a 180hp engine could power a 2,555lb airplane to speeds anywhere near 160mph until one trip I took in my 1960 Beech Debonair from San Jose, California, to El Paso, Texas, back in 1984. The Beech, with a Continental 225 up

In its day the Comanche was a world record-setting airplane in several distance categories, including a nonstop 7,668-mile hop from North Africa to Los Angeles, a 58hr flight. The basic aircraft accommodated four, but—as with this one—you could get six aboard some, and still get off the ground. Rated cruise was 182mph (75 percent power at 7,000ft). Standard fuel capacity was 60gal, with 90gal tanks an option (with 1,100 mile range). The Commanche series was built from 1958 until the flood at the plant washed out the tooling in 1972.

front, chugs along pretty close to 165mph, not bad for an old bird. We stopped for fuel in Tucson, Arizona, and that's where I met this couple traveling to El Paso in a Comanche 180.

Anyway, after telling the usual lies about how fast our respective planes would go on how little fuel, the idea of a point-to-point race came to mind. Seeing as how we were both headed to the same airport, we decided to make a small wager on the total time en route—the price of a good Mexican dinner at the El Parador Restaurant about 5 miles from El Paso International (ELP). We fired up within a minute of each other and, as agreed, started a stopwatch when I taxied out first, to be cleared to depart by Tucson Tower. After takeoff we were handed off to Tucson departure control and from there stayed on flight following for VFR advisories and to kind of keep track of where the other guy was. I tuned my second radio to 122.75 and was able to talk to the Comanche all the way to ELP. Good thing that I did. Otherwise, we might have run into each other on the 240-mile

---

Commanche Rating
Investment: #2 (All models have appreciated about the same percentages)
Utility: #4 (They are all heading into the classic status)
Popularity: #1 (I'll take a 400, thanks, replete with turbo)

---

cross-country. The flight lasted 1hr, 30min; when I was turning downwind to base, he was calling ELP tower for entry into the pattern. We started about 1min apart and he landed 1min behind me. Not too much difference for a supposed 45hp advantage. We flipped a coin for dinner. I lost that one too! The 180hp Comanche is the fastest general aviation airplane using the Lycoming O-360.

All the Comanches were equipped with a laminar-flow wing and retractable gear. Rather than go into a physics discussion about how a laminar-flow wing acts, suffice it to say that this type of wing has less drag than others. It also takes more hand labor to build, because tolerances are much more critical. The Piper Malibu is able to take advantage of this type of airfoil through the use of CAD/CAM design. If the Malibu had to be built with the same production techniques as the Comanche, it would cost about twice as much as it does now.

The Comanche was never a low-cost airplane. Hundreds of man-hours were spent fabricating individual pieces for each airframe.

The Comanche 180 was built at the same time as the Comanche 250, with the 180 at the lower end of the price scale. In 1958, $17,850 bought a well-equipped 180, while a Comanche 250 went out the door for $24,500. You have to remember what $24,000 would buy in 1958 to put these prices in perspective.

Comanche 400 Specifications

Engine: Lycoming IO-720-A1A, 400hp, 1,800hr TBO
Maximum Weight: 3,600lb
Fuel Capacity: 100gal (standard); 130gal (optional)
Maximum Speed at Sea Level: 223mph
Cruise Speed: 213mph
Range: 1,000nm at 75% power at 8,000ft (no reserve)
Fuel Consumption: 23.0gph
Rate of Climb at Sea Level: 1,600fpm
Service Ceiling: 19,500ft
Takeoff Ground Run: 980ft
Takeoff Over 50ft Obstacle: 1,500ft
Landing Ground Roll: 1,180ft
Landing Over 50ft Obstacle: 1,820ft
Stall Speed: 68mph (flaps extended)
Standard Empty Weight: 2,110lb
Maximum Useful Load: 1,490lb
Wing Span: 36ft
Length: 25ft 8in
Height: 7ft 3in

A real nice Hamilton diamond watch could grace a woman's arm for $89. A stereo TV (rare in 1958) had a $189.90 price tag. A 35ft Owens Cabin Cruiser, twin diesel engined and covered in Mahogany, sold new for $14,975. I could have been sent around the world on a six-week cruise for only $1,386. So laying out almost 25 large was a lot of money for an airplane. For that matter, it was a lot of money for a house!

Same thing prevails today. If Piper used modern technology and materials to build a

The Comanche was Piper's smallest high-performance single. Its retractable gear and laminar flow wing gave the Comanche surprising performance.

long range airplane with a laminar wing, it would cost a half-million dollars—same as the Malibu Mirage.

All the Comanches are excellent performers, the only problem is age. As I said above, the airplanes were almost completely hand built, one piece at a time. When a flood caused by hurricane Agnes caused the Susquehanna River to devastate the city of Lock Haven in 1972 and all the tooling was ruined, Piper took the opportunity to cancel

Comanches were built with 180hp, 250hp, 260hp, and 400hp Lycoming engines.

Comanche production. The cost of a 1972 Turbo C had passed the $50,000 mark, while a 1972 Seneca only brought $13,000 more. Piper was also fighting itself with the Arrow 200hp retractable and the Cherokee 235hp fixed gear, both four-place airplanes in the same market position as the Comanche.

Back in late 1962, two pilots from Traralgon, Australia, set out to find out how many hours a Comanche 180 could stay in the air. They donned heavy flying gear and oxygen masks, required at the high altitudes that they needed to reach to set a record for sustained flight in a single-engine airplane. Air Traffic Control (ATC) put an end to all their fun when they passed through 20,000ft, but the 180 was more than willing to go higher. Both pilots reported that "aircraft performance was at all times above reproach and, with an outside temperature of -28deg, the engine ran very sweetly. Cabin heater worked so well we both lost pounds in our protective clothing." This was quite a feat for 1962. Actually it would be a large accomplishment in 1993 to achieve the same altitude in a non-turbocharged airplane with 180hp. I made 15,300ft one day while fighting updrafts over the Sierra Nevadas between California and Nevada. The ground was only 4,000–5,000ft below me so it didn't look all that high, but my lungs were well aware of the 10min I spent up there. The Mooney 201 was not

Comanche 260 Typical Specifications
Engine: Lycoming O-540-E4A5, 260hp, 2,000hr TBO
Maximum Weight: 2,900lb
Fuel Capacity: 60gal (standard); 90gal (optional)
Maximum Speed at Sea Level: 194mph
Cruise Speed: 182mph
Range: 730nm at 75% power at 8,000ft (no reserve)
Fuel Consumption: 14.1gph
Rate of Climb at Sea Level: 1,500fpm
Service Ceiling: 10,600ft
Takeoff Ground Run: 760ft
Takeoff Over 50ft Obstacle: 1,040ft
Landing Ground Roll: 655ft
Takeoff Over 50ft Obstacle: 1,420ft
Stall Speed: 61mph (flaps extended)
Standard Empty Weight: 1,700lb
Maximum Useful Load: 1,200lb
Wing Span: 36ft
Length: 24ft 9 in
Height: 7ft 3 in

Comanche 260 B/C Typical Specifications
Engine: Lycoming IO-540-D4A5, 260hp, 2,000hr TBO
Maximum Weight: 3,100lb
Fuel Capacity: 60gal (standard); 90gal (optional)
Maximum Speed: 194mph at sea level
Cruise Speed: 182mph
Range: 730nm at 75% power at 8,000ft (no reserve)
Fuel Consumption: 14.1gph
Rate of Climb at Sea Level: 1,370fpm
Service Ceiling: 20,000ft
Takeoff Ground Run: 760ft
Takeoff Over 50ft Obstacle: 1,260ft
Landing Ground Roll: 655ft
Landing Over 50ft Obstacle: 1,435ft
Stall Speed: 61mph (flaps extended)
Standard Empty Weight: 1,728lb
Maximum Useful Load: 1,372lb
Wing Span: 36ft
Length: 25ft 3in
Height: 7ft 3in

doing much with its 200hp in the way of climbing at that point. The turbulence was getting more severe and big dark clouds were standing above all that granite in front of me, so my chicken factor forced me to perform a flawless 180 and return home. The only visiting I did in Reno that day was by phone.

The next model in the Comanche lineup was the Comanche 250. It was fitted with a carbureted Lycoming O-540 engine. Fuel injection, along with turbocharging, could be had as an option. With its wheels tucked up and the throttle well forward, the Comanche 250 could cruise 1,600 miles on 90gal optional tanks at 180mph. If you're looking for a classic airplane that also would take four people on a long cross-country for a reasonable fuel burn, the Comanche 250 should be among your first picks.

A 1958 model with low-time airframe and fairly new avionics can be had for $29,000. A real clean Comanche 250 with new everything and lots of modifications is asking $49,500, way over book value, but the owner says it's just like a new airplane from spinner to strobe. Comanches weren't normally used as trainers, and most of the people who bought a Comanche knew what they had and took excellent care of it.

A man named Maximum Conrad set a lot of nonstop distance records in a 250hp Co-manche. He flew from Casablanca to Los Angeles, 7,668 miles, without landing. Of course, then he had to turn around and take the airplane back to Casablanca so that later he could take a Comanche 180 from Casablanca to El Paso, 6,966 miles again nonstop.

Back in July 1961, Richard Collins, of *Flying* magazine fame, illustrated the Comanche's nonstop capability by detailing several long distance flights in a Comanche outfitted with 90gal tanks. Under prevailing wind and weather, point-to-point speed for one nonstop flight averaged 190mph; for another, 184mph.

Said a Piper dealer in Buenos Aires, "I simply climb to 20,000ft and go. At that level, using 39 percent power, I covered 1,240 miles. Groundspeed averaged 186mph and I landed with 3hr fuel remaining. A great flight and a great airplane."

Well, most of us will probably be satisfied with a cross-country of 400–500 miles. It's nice to know, though, that the airplane will go a lot farther than most people's bladders can comprehend. Casablanca to Los Angeles does make for some interesting flights of fancy. In reality, a well taken care of Comanche will be an excellent choice for long cross-country flights. Who knows, you might want to fly it from New York to Paris to arrive in time for the 1995 Paris Airshow. If you go, please drop a note to this author. I'd be happy to work the radios and run the GPS for the flight. I wouldn't eat much and I can tell lots of stories to help pass the time.

Then there's the Comanche 400. What to do when you want to be totally outrageous in an airplane. Only built from 1964–1965, this airplane was conceived by the same type of people who gave you the Pontiac GTO and the Dodge Hemi.

The Comanche 400 was a Comanche 250 that had been given a nose job and the new space underneath filled with a 720ci, eight-cylinder engine pumping out 400hp.

My kind of airplane.

A lot of hype was written in the early sixties about how the Comanche 400 could cover a lot of ground in a short time; how useful it could be in flying an executive to that next business meeting or conference without wasting precious time. Well, they had to justify putting 720ci of engine in an airplane that needed it about as badly as I need a third knee. I think the boys and girls at Piper were just like a lot of us—we like the push in the back and the rumble of horsepower when the throttle goes forward. It's a hot rod, pure and simple. Oh sure, the ads use words like "quietest at cruise," "smoother at altitude," and others of that ilk, but the real reason for the Super Comanche was power. Power to yank the airplane off the ground at 1,600fpm,

power to pull the plane through the air at 223mph flat out.

After putting all 400hp to work getting you off the ground in 980ft, the Comanche 400 would cruise along at 8,000ft with the power set at 65 percent, showing 213mph. If you're not put off by the 20gph fuel burn at 75 percent power, it's a real nice way to cover a lot of territory very quickly in a single-engine airplane. If you back down on the power to 55 percent (220hp) and fly at 12,000ft, you can cover over 1,000 miles with full reserves.

If I was going Comanche hunting, this airplane would definitely be at the top of my list. All is not beer and skittles, however, with the Comanche 400. If your engine runs past its TBO, expect to lay out $27,000 for the privilege of a rebuild. Also, these airplanes aren't exactly for sale at every airport. Not too many Comanche 400s came out of Lock Haven and of those that did, the numbers have been whittled down by age.

Expect to pay around $69,000 for a 1964 with 10hr on a fresh engine, new interior, and enough avionics to make a shuttle pilot jealous. Then there's the twin-turbo version of the 400. Some people figured that too much was just too little and worked out how to get a Supplemental Type Certificate (STC) to hang twin turbos on the engine. That way, you could play with 400hp all the way up to 12,000ft and carry 200mph up to 18,000ft. This

The Comanche 250 was powered by the 250hp 0-540 Lycoming engine with a 2,000hr TBO.

one will set you back at least $90,000, according to the latest ads. Plus it's going to take more care and feeding as you go along. Figure about double what it costs to run a Dakota and you'll be close—a little low, perhaps, but close. It's an airplane that I'd advise heavily to take to an FBO with mechanics who are real familiar with the 400, when it comes time to have a pre-purchase inspection. If I was the prospective buyer, I would budget at least one full day of an A&P's time to take the airplane apart for a real in-depth look. I'd probably throw in an oil change and a spark plug cleaning and gapping while the 400 was apart. When it looked like I was going to be the next owner, I'd increase the inspection to a full annual, even if it had been done within the last few months. I would stick closer to the mechanic than the skin on a basketball while he took off pieces and opened panels. I've learned that there is no such thing as too much maintenance, even if it just consists of taking a screwdriver for a walk around the airplane, looking and checking.

After having built a Harvard MK IV (T-6 Texan to those south of Canada) and a Cessna O-2A from a loose collection of parts to something that will fly you through the air, I have no problem spending a lot of time making sure the airplane is right. It's real hard to get out at 9,000ft to put a bolt in a gear door that's stopping the landing gear from extending. Since all the Comanches were manufactured before 1973, my math tells me that they are at least 20 years old. Think about taking a 1972 high-performance car out for a drive in 1993. If you are driving something flat out, say a Lamborghini Countach, a respectable fast car in the same league as a Comanche relative to performance and scarcity, you would like to know that all the pieces underneath you were going to stay in their assigned spots. Now convert that to a 20-year-old airplane 2 miles above the ground. Does all the talk about checking, checking, and checking again begin to make sense? After all, the pilot is always the first one at a crash and I have no desire to see either you or me in that position.

The Comanche 260 was probably the best all-around Comanche ever built. In all the various guises that it appeared—turbo, normally-aspirated, B-series, C-series, it was the

Comanche 260 Turbo C Specifications
Engine: Lycoming IO-540-N1A5, 260hp, 2,000hr TBO
Maximum Weight: 3,200lb
Fuel Capacity: 60gal (standard); 90gal (optional)
Maximum Speed: 195mph
Cruise Speed: 185mph
Range: 830nm at 75% power at 8,000ft (no reserve)
Fuel Consumption: 15.1gph
Rate of Climb at Sea Level: 1,320fpm
Service Ceiling: 25,000ft
Takeoff Ground Run: 820ft
Takeoff Over 50ft Obstacle: 1,400ft
Landing Ground Roll: 690ft
Landing Over 50ft Obstacle: 1,465ft
Stall Speed: 61mph (flaps extended)
Standard Empty Weight: 1,894lb
Maximum Useful Load: 1,306lb
Wing Span: 36ft
Length: 25ft 8in
Height: 7ft 3in

best in its class of single-engine retractables. The fuel injected Comanche 260 first appeared in 1965 as a replacement for the carbureted Comanche 250. Top speed was 195mph, with cruise a solid 185mph.

In 1966 the Comanche 260B was introduced. The fuselage was extended 6in over the earlier 260 and a third set of side windows were installed. The 260B could be ordered with the optional fifth and sixth seats, but anyone planning on spending much time in the last two seats had better be 3ft 6 in tall, or work as a body double for Plastic Man.

In 1969, probably the best of the Comanches was built, the 260C. The nose was changed to the elongated "shark" cowling, which many people think makes it the best looking airplane in the series. The standard price by then had risen to $42,500 fully equipped from an initial $30,740 for a 1965 C-260. Manually controlled turbocharging became available in 1970, allowing the 260C to maintain 185mph up at 18,000ft. Actual useful load on the Turbo 260C dropped from the 260B's and 260C's 1,372lb to 1,306lb without fuel, but the gross weight increased 100lb. The difference was in the turbo and related equipment—adding 158lb to the empty weight.

In appearance the 260C's rudder tip was slanted to resemble the Comanche 400's. The main gear went to a single fork strut to reduce drag in retracted position. It was powered by a stepped-up 260hp version of the Lycoming O-540 engine with fuel injection, making it an IO-540.

Inside, flying is more peaceful than in the 250. Piper installed the same double sound-proofing as found on the Twin Comanche and a new quieter dual exhaust system. The cabin is still loud by today's standards, but for the time, it was quite an improvement. Piper really wanted to stress comfort with the Comanche 260.

Improved shock mounts took a lot of vibration out of the engine. Inside, the seats were completely redesigned from the Comanche 250, and newer headrests and more cushy pillows were standard equipment. It was the first Piper single to feature individual fresh air and heater outlets for each seat. The heater size was increased to provide shirt-sleeve environment even in subzero outside temperatures.

Standard 60gal fuel capacity, carried in two 30gal wing tanks, gives the 260 a cruising endurance of almost 4hr at 185mph or a range of 730 miles, extended to 825 at economy cruise. With built-in reserve—including two optional 15gal wing tanks—range at 75 percent power is 1,120 miles and at economy cruise, in excess of 1,260 miles.

A wide choice of radio packages, autopilots, and other accessories were offered as factory options. The panel was set up for the IFR equipment popular at that time. With the advent of microprocessor-driven radios and navigation gear, most of the 20-year-old radios have been updated to modern equipment, such as Collins or King Nav/Coms and various lorans or GPS receivers.

There are a lot of modifications available for the Comanche series from a multitude of aftermarket airframe modifiers; such as one-piece windshields, speed breaks, door seals, center-stacked radios—replacing the earlier random placement—and so on. Every airplane that you check out will be a little different from the others. The price will pretty much be driven by the condition of the airplane rather than the year of manufacture. More and more, custom shops are locating good airframes and running them through an IRAN (inspect and repair as necessary) pro-

gram. *Trade-A-Plane* has six Comanche 260s and 400s, at various prices, that have been completely remanufactured. Expect the price to reflect the condition of the individual aircraft.

The 260C will probably hold its value better than the older types, especially if the Turbo C, with the Rajay turbocharger and manual wastegate, is the one you buy. Right now, a Turbo C will bring $6,000 more than the normally-aspirated 260C, coming in at $53,000 for a low-time, fully equipped airplane.

There's one for sale that spent all its life hangared and was only flown by a little old doctor on house calls—in Alaska—500 miles apart. He is willing to turn loose of his 260 Turbo C, 2,200hr TT since new, for the meager sum of $84,000—about $30,000 above book. Is it worth the asking price? You go look and let me know. Everything's negotiable, just make sure you know what you are buying.

Watch for the ADs on all Comanches. Some can get real expensive. I counted over sixty ADs covering 1958–1984. Not all apply to every airplane, but be sure and check to see that your prospective purchase has all of them complied with, especially the recurring ones.

Arrow and Turbo Arrow

In 1967, Piper began production of a four-place retractable called the Arrow. Initially it appeared with a 180hp Lycoming IO-360, 2,000hr TBO. In 1969 the engine's power was increased to 200hp using the same engine with cam and prop changes. The retractable-geared 180hp model enjoyed a 20mph increase over the Cherokee 180—a similar fuselage with fixed gear.

Prior to 1972, all the 200hp Arrows were referred to as the "B" series. After 1972 the Arrow II became standard with a 5in stretch in the cabin. Its 50gal fuel capacity gave it a 700-mile cruise range with full reserves. Its speed at 75 percent power was 165mph, while burning two-thirds the fuel of a comparable fixed-gear single.

In 1977 the Arrow III, still with the same 200hp Lycoming, but now with the Warrior II tapered wing, came on the scene. It was also the first offering of a Continental powered

TSIO-360 turbo engine. Still the same basic airframe, just ongoing improvements.

In actual operation, the Turbo Arrow and the Cessna Turbo Skylane RG will turn in almost the same speed average over a cross-country flight. Both will run along at 170kt at 20,000ft, making a 500nm trip in less than 3hr. The only airplane in the same class is the Mooney 231. Its turbocharged 200hp engine gives it a 190kt cruise speed. However, the Mooney gives up over 100lb useful load to the Turbo Arrow. Also, the Mooney fits most people like a leotard: it's more an airplane that you put on, as opposed to getting into.

Surprisingly enough, the useful loads of the Cessna Turbo Skylane RG and the Turbo Arrow IV aren't all that far apart. The Skylane has a 1,245lb useful load and the Arrow is only 37lb below it at 1,208. And the Turbo Arrow packs the load while burning 1.1gph less fuel than the Skylane.

Piper built the last in the series, the Arrow IV, as a T-tail and pushed its ability to go up high as a turbo version, or to just be a distinctively different airplane with the horizontal stabilizer and elevators stuck up on top of the tail. The looks certainly were different from the proceeding conventional-tailed Arrow III, but unfortunately so was the handling. At high angles of attack and low forward speed, as in landing configuration, the T-tail's airflow is partially blocked by the wing. Pitch control degrades with the lack of airflow over the horizontal surfaces, so more control input is required to make the airplane handle. Not quite the condition you want to see while 20ft above the ground on short final. Piper discontinued the Arrow IV in 1988, coming back on line with the Arrow III in 1989. Enough customers made enough noise about the T-tail to cause Piper to go back to the conventional airframe for the 1989 Arrow III. There were probably other reasons for changing, other than customer's wishes, but I imagine that pilots' opinions had a lot to do with it. Personally, I rather like the T-tail effect.

Evidently the engineers at Piper were real worried that pilots new to the Arrow would have a hard time remembering to put down the gear before they put down the airplane, so they designed a fail-safe method of ensuring that the rubber met the runway rather than

The first Arrow out of Piper's quiver was launched in 1967. The Arrow was a fully retractable single with a unique gear extension and retraction system. It was "Plane of the Year" for 1968: 180hp, 170mph top speed, 162mph cruise speed, 1,120lb of useful load, and an alleged range of 995 miles. This evolution of the basic Piper concept, with its wide-track retractable gear, has been through more makeovers and facelifts than a Hollywood starlet. This early airframe is probably worth about $35,000 in the current market, depending on condition and radios.

the prop tips reaching the asphalt first. Fully automatic gear, "The gear that thinks for itself," as Piper put it when introducing the Arrow B, is intended to save the pilot who forgets to extend the gear before landing. Piper knew that sometimes pilots tend to get a little distracted by everything surrounding an approach and landing to the point where little things get forgotten—like the gear. You can get away with forgetting to turn on the fuel pump; you can even make a landing look good if you don't lower the flaps; but it is real hard to cover up the fact that you just arrived with the wheels in the well. The scraping noises and the thwak-thwak-thwak as the prop hits the runway are dead giveaways. One highly embarrassed pilot even said, "I was so distracted by a warning buzzer that I forgot to put the gear down." As you might

---

Arrow and Turbo Arrow Rating
Investment: #2 (Rising, but others are rising faster)
Utility: #4 (Not a work plane)
Popularity: #2

The Arrow II variant was introduced in 1969, formally designated the PA-28R-200 (and then the 200B in 1972). The Arrow II is slightly longer than the original, a 5in stretch, and in 1974 the cabin interior was expanded to provide more space for the passengers. It is propelled by a 200hp Lycoming and is rated at a 165mph cruise.

guess, the warning buzzer was the gear-up alert.

The sequence of operation of the automatic gear goes like this. When the throttle is retarded and the airspeed drops to 105kt or slower, the gear warning horn blows. At the same time the gear automatically extends, even if the gear handle is in the retracted position.

The Arrow is one of the most difficult retractables to inadvertently bring in on its belly. This airplane puts the gear down whether you want it down or not, although as demonstrated here that is generally a good thing. Modifications to the nose wheel steering strut stops allow the aircraft to pivot in only a 13ft turning circle.

tion. Another automatic function of the gear retraction system is provided to guard against premature retraction on takeoff and accidental retraction while on the ground. What's more, a secondary, emergency free-fall manual gear extension is also provided to cover the slim possibility of a catastrophic power failure.

Can you see some of the less-than-pleasant features with auto gear? The worst would be becoming used to the gear working all by itself and relying on the airplane to do your job for you. Then you step into an airplane without the auto system—guess what's the outcome. Or if the auto system fails for some unbeknownst reason and you come sailing your merry way down final, thinking the airplane will extend the gear, only to have your revelry interrupted by the sounds of grinding airplane.

People who have done a gear-up landing say that the feeling you get between the time the airplane is at the point where the tires should touch down to the time the metal strikes the pavement can be the longest few seconds in your life. Always accompanied by that fine hollow feeling in the pit of your stomach, of course.

As this cutaway rendering shows, accommodations for passengers in Piper singles had come a long way since that first four-place cruiser back in the early sixties. The pilot's seat is now power operated, sound proofing is improved, and better ventilation makes the Arrow II " . . . a whole new experience to own and fly," according to Piper.

Another problem occurs when practicing stalls and minimum controllable airspeed maneuvers. When trying to do a power-off, gear-up stall and the gear keeps deploying, it's very tempting to pull all the breakers controlling the gear-warning system. There's a flashing light to remind you that the system is disabled, but, with a little more distraction, it can easily be missed. Then you forget to push the breakers back in. You're listening to the instructor shouting in your ear as the tower comes on the radio to change you to another runway, just when you normally would extend the gear. The warning horn's silent . . . more bent metal.

So, by now most of the flight schools have disconnected the auto gear and placarded the dash to so indicate. Now the Arrow

You can really rip right along in an Arrow once the automatic gear tucks itself back in the wells. The aircraft consumes about one-third less fuel than a fixed-gear aircraft with comparable performance. That works out to about a 700-mile range on 50gal of fuel at 165mph cruise.

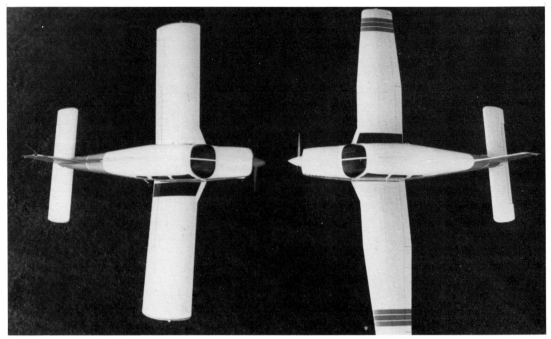

Despite what it looks like, this is not a precision mid-air collision but a comparison of the II and III models of the Arrow. The principal visible difference is the wing, longer and tapered in the Arrow III. Externally these aircraft are identical to fixed-gear Cherokee Warriors; parked side by side, an Arrow looks like a Cherokee without spats. The II was offered from 1972 to 1976, the III only during 1977 and 1978. The III was, unlike the II, a turbo.

operates just like any other retractable: you make the decisions, not the airplane. Now you're free to make your own mistakes.

The radio packages on the 1970s Arrows were set up in various groups to be sold at a package price. Usually King KX-170B or KX-175 B, Collins Com 11A or Com 111 radios were included in the full IFR group. The list of other optional equipment read like a laundry list from a Spanish coronation. Lots and lots of different goodies. Suffice it to say that no two Arrows on the used market will be equipped the same.

As with other Piper singles, the Arrow family came equipped with a multitude of options. Three different types of auto-pilots can appear in the panel. Piper AutoFlight II is Piper's basic automatic flight system. It keeps the plane straight and level, and makes standard-rate turns. Piper NavTracker II will couple to your radio, providing tracking on any desired VOR Omni course. Piper AutoControl III will let you select any course with its heading mode, integrated with the Directional Gyro (DG), and the Arrow will turn to and hold the desired course. The Roll Command knob provides turns up to 30deg of bank. With optional Omni Coupler, tracking on VOR radials with 15deg crosswind correction is provided as well as Omni and Instrument Landing System (ILS) localizer front and back course approaches. If some of this is hard to understand, stick with it—everything gets easier as the hours build.

When out shopping for an Arrow, as usual, inspect the logbooks. With a retractable airplane, there is always the chance of a gear-up or partial gear collapse landing. If the prop was pulled for any reason, prior to overhaul, check to see if there was a prop strike. Even if the engine was at a slow idle when the prop tips struck the runway, the engine has to come apart. The cases have to be split and the crank checked for cracks. Some pilots will just check the crank for runout with a dial indicator and if the crank is straight, put the prop back on and go fly. Where the trouble arises is when the airplane has acquired another few hundred hours and a new, uninformed owner.

The Turbo Arrow III is just a little longer than the II, but with a 200hp blown Continental engine and a two-blade constant speed prop. You can spot it by the slightly more pointed spinner, slightly different cowling, and an asking price that is likely to be quite different. This shot shows the Arrow III's somewhat extended nose and modified spinner. It is a similar aircraft to the Archer II, with retractable gear, a longer wing, and a more powerful engine. Inside that cowling is a turbocharged engine that will propel the Turbo Arrow III up to a 178kt maximum speed and a 172kt cruise, giving it a climb rate of almost 1,000fpm up to 20,000ft, and a maximum range of 895nm.

Arrow Typical Specifications

Engine:
1967—Lycoming IO-360-BE, 180hp, 2,000hr TBO
1969—Lycoming IO-360-C1C, 200hp, 2,000hr TBO
1977—Continental TSIO-360-F, 200hp, 1,400hr TBO
  (TSIO-360-FB, 1,800hr TBO)
All specifications below based on a 1979 Arrow III or
  Turbo Arrow III

Maximum Weight:
Arrow III—2,750lb
Turbo Arrow III—2,900lb

Fuel Capacity: 77gal

Maximum Speed:
Arrow III—152kt at sea level
Turbo Arrow III—178kt at 14,000ft

Cruise Speed:
Arrow III—143kt at 75% power at sea level
Turbo Arrow III—172kt at 75% power at 14,000ft

Range:
Arrow III—810nm at 75% power with 45min reserve;
  895nm at 55% power with 45min reserve
Turbo Arrow III—675nm at 75% power with 45min
  reserve; 740nm at 55% power with 45min reserve

Rate of Climb at Sea Level:
Arrow III—831fpm
Turbo Arrow III—940fpm

Service Ceiling:
Arrow III—16,200ft
Turbo Arrow III—20,000ft

Takeoff Ground Run:
Arrow III—1,025ft
Turbo Arrow III—1,110ft

Takeoff Over 50ft Obstacle:
Arrow III—1,600ft
Turbo Arrow III—1,620ft

Landing Ground Roll:
Arrow III—615ft
Turbo Arrow III—645ft

Landing Over 50ft Obstacle:
Arrow III—1,525ft
Turbo Arrow III—1,620ft

Stall Speed:
Arrow III—55kt (flaps extended)
Turbo Arrow III 57.5kt (flaps extended)

Standard Empty Weight:
Arrow III—1,601lb
Turbo Arrow III—1,663lb

Maximum Useful Load:
Arrow III—1,149lb
Turbo Arrow III—1,237lb

Wing Span: 35ft
Length: 25ft
Height: 8ft

Here's the Arrow IV, complete with T-tail, in a 1980 factory shot. The IV was introduced in 1977, replaced the III in 1980, then was discontinued in 1988—in favor of the III again! The tail configuration was a trendy design feature that turned out to create problems for slow-speed, high-angle-of-attack flight—short final approach kinds of situations. The design has been called a "Warrior II with a T-tail."

The value of any Arrow, from the early Is to late IVs (like this one), are quite variable. At this writing, Turbo IVs with comparable time and features are advertised at prices from about $48,000 to over $72,000. All of the Arrows are good airplanes—not extremely utilitarian, but durable, reasonably efficient, and sufficiently popular that you'll probably be able to unload it when you're done using it.

Usually if a cracked crank lets go, it's a big deal: the engine might break apart, the prop departs for places unknown, the airplane, hopelessly out of balance, spins down to crash.

Like I said—check the logs real carefully and have a mechanic who knows Arrows check your intended purchase closely. What you and I don't see, can be a glaring problem to some A&P mechanic who has spent the last ten years working on Pipers.

Now we come to one of my biggest stumbling blocks when it comes to buying an airplane—the price. I've owned eleven airplanes in the last fifteen years and don't think I could really afford any of them.

A 1970 Arrow 200 B that's been well maintained and kept in a hangar for most of its life will fetch about $35,000; more for extra avionics or low TT. I found two 1979 Turbo Arrow IVs, one with 845hr TT and a REMAN engine installed 250hr ago, the other with 2,800hr TT and 1,290hr SMOH. Both had comparable equipment and radios. The first owner was asking $72,000 and the second wanted $47,500 for his airplane. The only way that you can tell if one airplane is worth that much more than the other, is to go look at them. My selection would have to be dollar driven, unfortunately. However, if you just came into your second trust fund or the lottery paid you this year's installment on the $24 million you won, then I'd say go pick the best airplane money can buy. Either way, none of the Arrows, from the first 180hp 1967 to the 1991 Turbo Arrow IV, has a bad bone in its body.

Malibu and Malibu Mirage

The Piper Malibu is a 310hp pressurized single capable of speeds and altitudes more common to twins. First seen in 1984 with a

Continental TSIO-520 providing motivation, the Malibu was plugged as the fastest piston-engine airplane in production. Its speed of 187kt above 18,000ft for 1,500nm proved that to be true, and people lined up to buy them.

In 1986, among all new aircraft delivered between January and March of that year, only the Cessna 172 and the Mooney 231 left their respective factories in larger numbers than did the Piper Malibu, and the 231 by only one unit.

At a 1986 selling price of $376,105, Piper's Malibu is also the most expensive piston-powered single on the market: exceeding the Cessna pressurized 210 by almost $75,000. Even during the depressed market times, dealers were able to sell Malibus at or slightly above list. In November 1993, a new Malibu Mirage lists for over $550,000.

The Malibu is a six-place, pressurized business single that came out in 1983. It is the first piston-powered single to offer a pressurized cabin. The plain vanilla version is powered by a 310hp Continental; later airframes had Lycoming engines installed and are known as the Malibu Mirage. *Lafferty Aircraft Sales*

Piper's use of computer-aided design and computer-aided manufacturing (CAD/CAM) allowed the company to produce very efficient structural designs. Better designs through CAD/CAM allowed Piper to fabricate a high aspect ratio wing (11:1), without the high weight penalty usually associated with the supporting structures. Also, the aluminum skin is milled to 0.032in thick, in contrast to the Cessna 210 at 0.020in. The thicker skin allows the fuselage to be made smoother

Malibu and Mirage Specifications

Engine:
Malibu—Continental TSIO-520-BE, 310hp, 2,000hr TBO
Mirage—Lycoming TIO-540-AE2A, 350hp 2,000hr TBO
All specifications below based on a 1986 Malibu with average equipment
Maximum Ramp Weight: 4,118lb
Maximum Takeoff Weight: 4,100
Maximum Landing Weight: 3,900lb
Zero Fuel Weight: 3,900lb
Fuel Capacity: 122gal (120gal usable)
Maximum Speed: 234kt
Cruise Speed: 215kt at 75% power
Long Range Cruise: 196kt at 55% power
Range: 1,330nm at 75% power with 45min reserve; 1,555nm at 55% power with 45min reserve
Pressurization: 7,900ft at 25,000ft with 5.5psi
Rate of Climb at Sea Level: 1,143fpm
Service Ceiling: 25,000ft
Takeoff Ground Run: 1,440ft (20deg flaps)
Takeoff Over 50ft Obstacle: 2,025ft
Landing Ground Roll: 1,070ft
Landing Over 50ft Obstacle: 1,800ft
Stall Speed: 58kt (40deg flaps); 68kt (flaps up)
Maximum Useful Load: 1,652lb
Wing Span: 43ft
Length: 28.4ft
Height: 11.3ft

As befits an airplane that costs as much as a Malibu—$250,000 and up at this writing—passenger accommodations are reasonably comfortable. Piper offered a variety of upholstery fabrics for the seats. *Lafferty Aircraft Sales*

This clean, neat Malibu is waiting for its next owner in the Lafferty Aircraft Sales hangar. Particularly for Pipers in this price class, brokers offer some substantial advantages for most buyers. Brokers share a computer network that links buyers and sellers all over the world with each other, offering a lot more choices than even publications like *Trade-A-Plane* provide. *Lafferty Aircraft Sales*

and hold down the number of drag-inducing wrinkles and waviness on the upper surfaces of the wing and tail, maintaining a smooth contour and lowering drag.

Even though the skin is thicker and the wing has a higher aspect ratio than the C-210's wing, the Malibu tips the scales at 4,100lb, the same weight as a 210 Centurion, its only competition in the pressurized-singles class. With a stronger fuselage, the Malibu is

It seems that every panel is different, one way or another. This one has essentially the standard factory panel with HSI, DME, KX 155 radios, ADF and gyro, but with great tunes on that stereo cassette on the bottom of the radio stack. The sheepskin seat covers ought to add a couple of grand to the sticker price, too. *Lafferty Aircraft Sales*

able to use 5.5psi of pressurization, giving it a cabin altitude of 7,000ft when the airplane is at 23,000ft. The Cessna is limited by older design to a cabin pressure differential of 3.4lpsi, holding it to lower altitudes. The Malibu's cruise speed is within 25kt of the fastest cabin-class twin, the Cessna 421, and its runway requirements are less than all other cabin twins.

You and five friends can load up a Malibu with fuel and luggage on a Friday after work, light the fire, and depart to a destination 1,000 miles away while enjoying the comfort of flying at 25,000ft, above most of the bad weather. The cabin altitude will be at 7,000ft, so no need to wear awkward oxygen masks. Holding a conversation will be no problem during the flight because pressurization makes for a quieter cabin, so there is less noise-induced stress to tire you out during the less-than 5hr flight time to cover your 1,000nm trip.

Most Malibus came from the factory with a full panel of IFR avionics as a standard package. When you ordered a Malibu, unless you specified something else, the airplane came with two King KX-165 radios, a King ADF, DME, Transponder, autopilot, compass system, and a Narco Emergency Locator Transmitter (ELT). The package included avionics master switch, electric longitudinal trim, microphone, speaker, headset, two sets of phone jacks, and static discharge wicks. The new owner could option for a second glideslope, a second transponder, RNAV, autopilot coupling, and DME.

Actually, the airplane could be had with just about anything your checkbook could cover. If you wanted a weatherscope, three were available. You could talk to the office while reclining in the cabin with a Wulfsburg Flitefone II with WH-10 handset for the measly cost of $8,205 in 1986. Of course, the panel could be filled with lorans, GPS, and other long-range navigational equipment. It's just a matter of money.

Piper did have some trouble with the Malibu during the first few years of operation. The problem was thought to be with a runaway autopilot, causing loss of control of the airplane. Later the airplane was exonerated; investigation by the FAA and others laid the blame at the pilots' feet. The rational was that pilots weren't sufficiently trained in the airplane, so if something went wrong, they were unable or too slow to handle the problem. All the Malibus were grounded in 1989 until Piper and the government figured out what was going on.

Piper knew that this would be a large inconvenience for those pilots who had already scheduled a flight for vacation or business purposes, so the aircraft manufacturer offered to buy first-class tickets for any Malibu owners inconvenienced by the grounding.

This was fine as it goes; however, it wasn't a lot of help to a friend of mine who had his Malibu lose its engine while in flight, back in 1989. He had departed Reid-Hillview Airport near San Jose, California, heading southeast, straight out from Runway 12R. The trip was to be of long duration, involving climbing over some high mountains, so he was climbing hard to a cruise altitude up in the 23,000ft range. About 11 miles out from the field, the engine let go with enough force to blow all the oil out of the sump, a large portion landing on the windshield. The engine was so badly blown that the prop had locked up solid and would not turn. Later investigation showed a rod through the side of the crankcase, wedging the crank from rotating.

The Malibu had gained enough altitude by that time to make it back to the airport for a dead-stick landing, or so my friend thought. He could only see clearly out of the left side window, as the windscreen was covered with Shell's best 20w-50 oil, rendering forward vision poor to zilch. After he turned (*very* gently) back towards the airport and set up a best-rate glide, he had time to call the tower and inform them of his minor problem. One of the nicer features of Reid-Hillview's approach from the south is that a developer got the city to let him build a shopping mall right at the end of the airport boundary. When landing on Runway 31 on a hot day, your airplane experiences a small bump as it passes over the hot air given off by the air conditioning condensers on the roof of the Penney's department store. Gene knew that he was going to have to arrive rather hot and high to ensure that he didn't make an unscheduled arrival in the second floor ladies department of Penney's.

By now he had settled down somewhat, meaning his heart was no longer pressing up against his sinus cavities. The return glide was going to be quicker than the departure, but he still had about 5min to worry through before he arrived at the runway. He held the gear until he was sure that he'd make the airport. As he crossed the airport boundary, Gene threw in all the flaps and planted it within 50ft of the end of the asphalt. All this while only being able to see clearly out the left side window. The Malibu slid down 31R with both brakes smoking and the tires leaving long black lines the entire length of the runway. If this was a TV adventure, he would have slid off the end only to stop up against the fence at the edge of airport property. In real life, the airplane smoked almost 2,900ft down the runway, managing to stop with less than 10ft of pavement left. When I saw the airplane shortly after it landed and before the tires could be changed, it was hard to recognize what type of airplane sat under all that oil. About eight quarts had blown out of the cowl, covering the Malibu from windshield to wings. Gene allowed as how it might be awhile before he went up in that particular plane again. The engine was replaced by Piper, and nothing much was ever said about why it let go.

An almost identical panel to the previous one—until you discover the color radar. Malibus have largely taken over the light-twin market. Previously, you would probably be looking for a twin-engine Seminole or Beech Duke for the kind of applications that many people buy single-engine Malibus for today, thanks to improved single-engine reliability. *Lafferty Aircraft Sales*

One Zero Niner Mike is just passing through about 150ft AGL with 10 degrees of flaps (first notch) and with the gear lever freshly placed in the UP position. The nose gear stows first, the mains follow in the Malibu.

But now it's 1993 and I'm scheduled to go up in the same plane to shoot some pictures for this book. Yes, I'm looking forward to the flight. The only problem I might have is giving the Malibu back to the owner when the photo shoot is over.

In 1988 Piper dropped the Lycoming TIO-540 twin-turbocharged, intercooled, 350hp engine in the Malibu, renaming it the Malibu Mirage. From what owners have to say, the Malibu Mirage is everything the original airplane should have been. With Lycoming's 40hp advantage over the Continental engine in the Malibu, the Mirage gains mostly in time to altitude with a smaller advance in cruising speed. At 25,000ft the Mirage will cruise at 225kt, climbing there better than 1,200fpm. The gross weight is up to 4,300lb, a 200lb increase over the Malibu's gross, for a useful load of 1,692lb. The optional ice protection package, including a new integrally heated windshield, allows flight into known-ice conditions.

Two 70-amp, 28-volt alternators and a split-bus electrical system provide plenty of energy for the Mirage's electrical and avionics requirements throughout any IFR flight. Piper also offers the new owner of a Mirage an indepth flight-training program at its headquarters in Vero Beach, Florida. Classes are conducted frequently and include ground schools as well as a flight transition program.

The Malibu and the Mirage are a tough act to follow, when it comes to flying a cabin class single. They're stiff competition for a lot of cabin twins, for that matter. What little time I have in one sure convinced me it's the way to fly.

The first 1984 Malibu sold for $320,000. Today a nice 1984 will bring $215,000, but watch the time on the fuselage and wing. The fuselage is life-limited to 10,145hr and the wing to 15,580hr, so a high-time airplane will be worth considerably less. Like all the other Pipers, the Malibu keeps stepping up in price as the years get newer, with a pre-owned 1989 Mirage bringing $340,000, and the newest one I could find on the market, a 1991, bringing 100 percent of its new retail, $532,800.

Strange thing. The Piper single to own for 1964 was the Comanche 400, with a 400hp Lycoming up front. Today it costs about $27,000 to rebuild its engine. The new, hotrod Mirage's 350hp Lycoming runs almost the same price when overhaul time rolls around. Speed seems to cost the same, no matter the year.

Chapter 5

The Working Indians

Cherokee Six

Let's say you want to start an aerial piano moving company, but you don't have enough money for a new Cessna Caravan. What airplane would you pick? Well, if I was in the cheap piano moving air-freight business, I'd probably opt for one of the Cherokee Sixes. The "small" one has 260hp, room for six people, and a real-life load of 1,300lb. The bigger Six, the 300hp model, can carry 84gal of fuel, six people, and enough luggage for a three-week trek to Nepal. Plus it will yank all that load off an unimproved grass strip in a little over 1,000ft. Then, either one can stay aloft

The PA-32 Cherokee Six was designed to turn the basic low-wing design into something of a cargo aircraft, and succeeded. It was first offered in 1965 and production lasted until 1979.

until we go back on Daylight Savings Time.

Both Sixes are relatively simple airplanes, fixed gear, constant-speed prop and the same big wing of the PA-28 series. They are basically stretched Cherokee 235s with bigger en-

You can get a Six in either 260hp or 300hp versions. The latter has fuel injection and the factory claimed 174mph for a top speed, 168mph cruise. Both will carry up to seven people or a lot of cargo. If you pull the seats out you've got 110cu-ft of cargo capacity, plus performance that will get the thing airborne with 1,300lb of payload plus pilot and 50gal of fuel. Maximum useful load was rated at 1,717lb with the seats out.

Cherokee Six 260 Typical Specifications
Engine: Lycoming O-540-E4B5, 260hp, 2,000hr TBO
Maximum Weight: 3,400lb
Fuel Capacity: 50gal (standard); 84gal (optional)
Maximum Speed: 168mph
Cruise: 160mph
Fuel Consumption: 18.5gph
Range: 510nm (standard tanks)
Rate of Climb at Sea Level: 850fpm
Service Ceiling: 12,800ft
Takeoff Ground Run: 1,200ft
Takeoff Over 50ft Obstacle: 1,800ft
Landing Ground Roll: 640ft
Landing Over 50ft Obstacle: 1,000ft
Stall Speed: 47mph
Standard Empty Weight: 1,784lb
Maximum Useful Load: 1,616lb
Wing Span: 32.8ft
Length: 27.7ft
Height: 8.2ft

gines. The 260 and the 300 share the same airframe, only difference being 40hp. The 300hp model came out one year after the 260 appeared in 1965; both were out of production in 1979, just prior to the Saratoga's introduction in 1980.

In real numbers, the Cherokee Six 260, with six 170lb people on board and 200lb of baggage distributed between the nose compartment and the aft cargo area, will burn 14gph while making 133kt over an 800-mile route. Or you can play the fuel-versus-cargo game to the point of putting a 900lb Caterpillar Tractor engine head in the space usually taken by the third and fourth passenger, fill 3hr worth of fuel in the tanks, then haul the load back to a gravel strip next to a gold mine in Alaska near Mt. Denali National Park.

Yes folks, I was there, back in 1978 when the mining company stuffed the Cherokee with Caterpillar parts. No, I wasn't the pilot, I stood on the side of the runway waiting for the engine head to fall through the belly of the airplane when the forklift backed away. Very

This cutaway gives some idea of the massive volume of the Six's cabin. The seating was still a bit Spartan, but there was room for a lot of folks in there.

All Sixes came with double doors that provided a 5ft-wide opening into the cabin for convenient stowage of bulky cargo—or unruly kids, as in this shot.

anticlimactic. The mine foreman told me I should be around when they put a *real* load in the Cherokee. Right!

The pilot later told me that the gold-mining company flew that airplane almost daily throughout the short summer months hauling everything from beer to warm bodies. The rough end of the trip was a gravel landing strip a whole 2,100ft long. It had been hacked out of the river bank as far as the tractor could cut without putting a 30-degree turn in the runway. Oh, and it was a one-way strip. You landed going towards a 2,000ft ridge and departed the other way, over the river. Tim, the pilot for the mine, said that sometimes the strip got to looking real short when the wind wasn't quite right. He thought it was real funny to see the looks on the faces of the mine worker passengers after he shut down with 5–6ft left of the runway. He said that more than once, he had to kill the engine, then use the towbar to turn around at the end of the runway. Sometimes he got his feet a little wet when he had to step back a ways into the river to hook the towbar. That type of flying made it clear to me that my desire to fly bush pilot in Alaska was doomed to failure.

They told me that after a season in Alaska, the airplane spent winter in Seattle getting IRANed. Everything that could come apart, came apart. The airplane was almost totally rebuilt before the summer returned.

The moral of the story should be clear to anyone thinking about making a Cherokee Six their next airplane. Look at the logs first. The airplane sitting in front of you may look real pretty with a new paint job and perfect upholstery, but it may have spent its entire life hauling heavy equipment out of unimproved gravel strips. The reason the seats look so good is they spent all their life in a plastic bag in the back of an unheated hangar in Chichagof, Alaska (summer population 16, not including seals).

A lot of the Cherokee 260s and 300s spent their entire life paying their way. Not that that's an automatic disqualifier when it comes to making a choice, but I think I'd rather have one that never had its seats pulled and plywood laid down on the deck. I did see a Cherokee 300 for sale that had spent ten years of its life having people fall out of it. For a skydiving airplane, it was in pretty good shape. Wear around the hatch edges, but no more than expected.

The neat thing about both Cherokee Sixes is the compound cargo door behind the wing on the pilot's side. The main entry door will open to the left to access the rear four seats. If a wider load than the standard door can handle needs to be loaded, then the utility door on the right can be raised, giving a total of 4ft of width. Even leaving in the conference-style rear seats (facing each other) doesn't diminish

Cherokee Six 300 Typical Specifications
Engine: Lycoming 10-540-K1G5D, 300hp, 2,000hr TBO
Maximum Weight: 3,400lb
Fuel Capacity: 50gal (standard); 84gal (optional)
Maximum Speed: 156mph
Cruise Speed: 152mph
Fuel Consumption: 18gph
Range: 652nm (standard tanks)
Rate of Climb at Sea Level: 1,050fpm
Service Ceiling: 16,250ft
Takeoff Ground Run: 900ft
Takeoff over 50ft Obstacle: 1,350ft
Landing Ground Roll: 630ft
Landing over 50ft Obstacle: 1,000ft
Stall Speed: 55mph
Standard Empty Weight: 1,846lb
Maximum Useful Load: 1,554lb
Wing Span: 32.8ft
Length: 27.7ft
Height: 8.2ft

the 17cu-ft of cargo space in the aft section of the airplane.

I once met a young couple who were spending their honeymoon in a Cherokee 300, roaming around the southwestern part of the United States. They had pulled all four rear seats, turning the airplane into a camper. A cook stove, propane lantern, sleeping bag, and all the bits and pieces necessary to camp out inhabited the rear cabin. In good weather, they strung hammocks from the wing tiedowns to nearby trees. On a cooler night, they used the airplane's battery to power a small air compressor to blow up an air mattress. The husband said keeping the cook stove fueled up was no problem with 84gal of fuel less than 10ft away. He said that so far, the 100 LL avgas had worked just fine in the stove. They had been married two weeks less than they had owned the Cherokee, and they were talking about using it as a flying camper for years to come.

Transitioning into a Cherokee Six from a four-place Piper isn't all that difficult. The control forces are heavier, the airplane can't be thrown around like a Warrior, and the power management takes a little getting used to; especially if you've never flown a constant-speed prop. Part of making the big six respond properly on landing is to carry a little power until the runway almost grabs the wheels. If you fly a Six like a light twin, then you won't have any trouble with it.

One surprise, transitioning from 180hp to 300hp, will be filling the tanks. This event will happen more often than it did in your trusty Cherokee 180 and it will dig farther into your wallet. At today's avgas prices, squirting 70–80gal into the tanks will set you back a good $170. Fuel prices will put a premium on learning proper leaning of the engine for maximum range. This is when an exhaust temperature gauge (EGT) comes in handy. At cruis-

One of the things you can stow aboard a Six is a big ferry fuel tank, something that probably helped this one win the 1976 Powder Puff Derby.

Cherokee Six 260s were produced from 1965 to 1978 and were delivered with Lycoming O-540-E4B5 engines with 2,000hr TBOs. Maximum weight was rated at 3,400lb, fuel capacity was 50gal standard/80 optional, and the Six could cruise at 160mph. Fuel consumption is rated at 18.5gph, range is 510nm, and service ceiling is 12,800ft.

Cherokee Six 300s were built from 1966 to 1979 and were delivered with Lycoming O-540-K1G5D engines with 300hp and 2,000hr TBOs. Maximum speed is 156mph, cruise is 152mph, range is 652nm, and service ceiling is 16,250ft.

ing altitude, pull back the mixture until the EGT peaks. Then push in the control for a 50-degree drop. This setting will give best power. If your handbook shows a slightly different method—go with the book.

The 300hp Lycoming IO-540 will operate within a wide power range. Flying at 55 percent power, with the engine leaned to best economy, will produce a fuel burn of 12gph. You will only be covering ground at 129kt, but you can travel over 900 miles between fuel stops. A more realistic power setting of 65 percent will true out to 140kt, with a fuel burn of 14gph at best economy, or 16.1gph at best power gaining a 5mph increase.

When it comes to pricing a Cherokee Six, in general, the 260hp model will bring $7,000–9,000 less than its 300hp brother. A semi-low-time 260, say 1967–1972 year range, will bring between $29,000 and $46,000. The same year span for a 300 comes in at $34,000 to $50,000. The year of the airplane isn't what drives the price, so much as the condition of the airframe and time on the engine. A 1977 IO-540, as in the Cherokee 300, will run $19,000 to overhaul, not counting accessories. The same overhaul on the 260 engine will be $14,000, a $5,000 savings. The big engine is in-

jected, which adds a bit to the rebuild if the injection unit needs to be rebuilt or replaced. The Cherokee 260 sports a carburetor, cheaper to rebuild, but not as efficient.

What do you want to look at in a Cherokee Six prior to autographing a check? As mentioned above, read the logbooks carefully. When checking under the cowl, pay particular attention to the firewall. Wrinkles or added pieces of sheet metal are a sure sign that someone tried to make a wheelbarrow out of the airplane. Sometimes this is accompanied by a prop strike, so make sure that if a hard nose landing is evident or a prop strike shows in the logbook, the engine was taken apart and the crankshaft Magnafluxed or X-rayed for cracks. As mentioned before, a cracked crank might not make itself evident for a few hundred hours or more. Usually following Murphy's law, the crank will let go when you need it the most. It's real easy to repair a broken part in a hangar on a sunny day. Doing anything more than recriminations is very hard in the middle of a flight in hard IFR conditions.

If you take a real close look at the actual useful load difference between the 260 and the 300, you'll see that less than 100lb separate the two. In 1977, the Cherokee 260 actually had a higher useful load than the 300, 1,616lb to 1,544lb for the 300. Actual carrying capacity will vary, depending on as-equipped weight of the two airplanes; which one gets the lead depending on weight and balance. The cruising speeds only differ by 15–20kt, so if absolute speed isn't necessary, then the 260 might be a better choice. Whichever you decide to buy, have it gone over thoroughly, and remember, check the logs, watch for corrosion, and go start your own aerial moving company.

Lance

In 1976, Piper introduced the retractable model of the Cherokee Six 300, the PA-32 Lance. The Lance shared the same fuselage as the 300 until late in the 1978 model year, when the T-tail appeared on the Lance. All the Lances used the "Hershey-Bar" wing construction. The 1978 Lance caused quite a bit of dissent and discussion when the T-tail appeared. The shift away from the standard tail was more a styling move than anything else. It turned out to be the biggest reason for sales resistance for the Lance II, the first T-tail model.

The problem centers around performance, or the lack thereof. The paper performance figures for the Lance and Lance II show the same takeoff run for both airplanes. Most pilots will disagree with published figures, saying that the Lance II takes quite a bit more runway to lift off. I have talked to pilots

who have flown both airplanes and the comments reflect a difference of 500–600ft in take-off run. Also, a few pilots say that the airplane has a pitch problem upon rotation, tending to come off the nose gear quite suddenly. Instructors who teach uprating into the Lance II say that it is more a perceived problem than one of actual over-rotation. On landing, the wing does tend to block some of the airflow over the tail, making for a change in control input just prior to touching down. The landings are more a case of getting accustomed to what the airplane does rather than a change in control. The T-tail Pipers have a different feeling than the straight tail versions, mostly evident in takeoff.

The Lance is similar to the Cherokee Six in that it will haul quite a load quite a distance. You can pack five people and full fuel in the airplane and stay in the air far past standard bladder duration. By pulling back to 55 percent power, the Lance will burn 11.9gph with the engine leaned to best economy. That works out to 864nm, 6.3hr of flying.

Very few pilots will opt to drone along at under 140kt in a 300hp airplane. After all, one of the biggest reasons people turn into pilots is to fly somewhere faster than they can drive. Usual power settings will be closer to 65 per-

The original Lance was essentially a Cherokee Six 300 with retractable gear. It has a conventional tail and was first flown in 1974. It was produced from 1976 until 1978. The design uses the conventional "Hershey-Bar" wing and, until 1978, the conven-

tional tail layout. The Lance is a working airplane, designed to haul the same heavy load of people or cargo that will fit in the Cherokee Six—a lot, up to 1,620lb useful load. Its rated cruise is 158kt, fuel consumption is 18gph, and range is 900 miles.

cent, or 149kt. At that speed, a trip from Seattle to San Francisco will take 3.8hr nonstop, using 64gal of fuel in flight. With 10gal figured for start-up, taxi, takeoff, and light headwinds, that still leaves a reserve of almost 20gal.

The Lance is at its best flying missions similar to those flown by the Cherokee Six. Two- or three-hour flights with a load of six people or a half-ton of cargo, seems to be the best use of the airplane.

The actual cruise speed difference between the Cherokee 300 and the Lance is only around 8kt, depending on power setting. You will have to decide if the speed increase and the look of a smooth belly is worth the additional maintenance brought on by retractable gear. As the airplane ages, the repair costs on the gear will increase. One repair problem brought on by the landing gear can eat up a

lot of the savings gained with an 8kt cruise advantage. Now that the airplane has been out of production since 1979, parts are getting harder to find. With Piper in and out of bankruptcy back in 1991, when it only had $1,000 in cash and forty-five employees, not too many parts were shipped to the few dealers that remained. An owner of a Seminole had to resort to welding over previous welds to repair a lower tube on the main gear because parts were and are nonexistent. Sifting through aircraft salvage yards only turned up

Piper promoted the Lance's tail-high ground attitude as an aid to visibility during ground handling operations.

A rather large scoop on the left side of the Lance's cowling feeds ram air into the engine's air intake. Piper claimed this maximized horsepower and contributed to the aircraft's performance and load handling.

one set of lowers, that the owner wouldn't separate, for an asking price of $600. Two years ago, I had an experience when my airplane (not a Piper) got a bad case of stuck gear. Luckily it was stuck down, so no big

---

Lance Typical Specifications

Engine: Lycoming IO-540-K1G5D, 300hp, 2,000hr TBO
Maximum Weight: 3,600lb
Fuel Capacity: 98gal
Maximum Speed: 165mph
Cruise Speed: 158kt
Fuel Consumption: 18gph
Range: 900 miles
Rate of Climb at Sea Level: 1,000fpm
Service Ceiling: 14,600ft
Takeoff over 50ft Obstacle: 1,660ft
Takeoff Ground Run: 960ft
Landing over 50ft Obstacle: 1,708ft
Landing Ground Roll: 880ft
Stall Speed: 52kt (flaps extended)
Standard Empty Weight: 1,980lb
Maximum Useful Load: 1,620lb
Wing Span: 32.8ft
Length: 27.8ft
Height: 9ft

---

deal. Unluckily it cost $1,600 by the time the shop had spent three days adjusting and swinging the gear. The total parts bill consisted of two squat switches at $49 each. So think over your choice before spending the extra money for the retractable.

Because of the above reasons, Lances formerly sold for less than a Cherokee Six, but with the demise of the small aircraft market, it seems as though the Lance has outlived its reputation. A good 1976 Lance with 1,094hr TT is being offered at $69,500, an increase of about 20 percent in the last four years. Admittedly, it is a Turbo, a model we'll discuss in the next segment. It still proves the point that a good airplane will bring good money.

Now seems like an appropriate time to discuss ongoing costs. When you buy your Lance, Dakota, Saratoga, or Cheyenne 400 LS, the cost of operating the airplane has to be calculated into the yearly operating cost along with the loan payment on the airplane.

These costs are:

Annual fixed expenses, including tie-down fees of $77 per month ($924 per year), insurance premium of $2,880 per year (hull and liability with $500 deductible at $500,000 single limit)—a total of $3,804. If you fly 500hr per year, annual fixed expenses will cost you $7.60 per hour

Operating expenses per hour, including fuel at $30.87 (14.7gph at $2.10 per gallon), oil at $1.80 per quart, annual inspection at $11.50 ($5,750), engine exchange at $17.50, prop overhaul at $1.85, and Avionics-maintenance reserve (this one's tough to estimate) at $2.20—a total operating expense per hour of $65.72 on a 1977 Lance.

Add the two together, and you get the total hourly operating expense of $73.32. This is in addition to the payment on the airplane, any unexpected maintenance, landing fees or tiedown fees at other airports and unusual expenses, such as refilling the oxygen system. All these costs are based on rates current as of November 1993 at local shops in the San Francisco area.

Bear in mind that the annual inspection, figured at $5,750, could run higher, but very seldom lower. All in all, the cost to operate an airplane the size of a Lance can easily run over $1,200 per month if your loan has a seven-year payback. All this has to be considered when thinking about purchasing such a complex airplane.

You can use these figures to estimate the operating cost of any airplane before you buy. Just plug in the numbers and see what comes up. Remember, these numbers are based on flying an airplane 500hr per month. If you fly fewer hours yearly, the per hour cost will go up, because all the fixed costs—annual, avionics repair, hangar, and so on—stay the same. If you fly only 100hr per year, per hour cost for the annual will jump to 5,750. The tie-down fee and insurance will take $38 per hour, five times as much.

So, before you lay any money on the table, it might behoove you to run through this drill to see if the airplane of your dreams will remain that way, or will it be too expensive?

Turbo Lance II

Piper decided to make the Lance a Turbo in 1978. The only visual difference is the air intake at the lower front of the cowl. To those of us with a twisted sense of humor, the air inlet gives rise to many imaginative mental shapes. It does do what it's intended to do and that's help ram in air to the Lycoming TIO-540.

The Turbo is capable of taking off from a 2,500ft strip with a load of six passengers and 200lb of luggage and can climb to 10,000ft in less than 10min. Set up best-power cruise and watch your airplane true out at over 170kt. Climb to 20,000ft, to top weather or mountains, for even faster airspeeds. Depending on the winds aloft, the Turbo Lance can scoot along, showing over 200kt groundspeed. Quite a considerable advance over the Cherokee Archer or Warrior that you were renting before. The Turbo will make many trips nonstop on which you used to have to plan at least one fuel stop in a smaller plane. Some-

The Lance II adopted the T-tail in 1978—the first year of production. Turbocharged Lances were also offered that year for the first time; this configuration is supposed to provide a few extra miles per hour through lower drag. It has also provided a lot of dubious remarks from the field about that performance, particularly when the nose is up and the speed and gear is down as the plane slides down the glide path toward the numbers.

The Lance has an airspeed-sensor probe that is mounted to the left side of the fuselage. At about 115mph an automatic system extends the gear; the same system retracts it after 95mph airspeed is attained on takeoff. The whole system has its own electro-hydraulic system to let you get the wheels down, even if the aircraft's main systems somehow fail.

Turbo Lance II Rating
Investment: #3
Utility: #2
Popularity: #3 (Some love them; some wouldn't use them for flower planters)

A 300hp blown Lycoming powerplant and oversized air intake on the lower front of the engine cowl are the only way to distinguish the Turbo II from other Lances.

times spending more money to go high and fast is, overall, the most economical way to fly.

Be sure to check the turbocharger and its related parts, brackets, and oil lines very carefully in a pre-purchase inspection. Actually, if I was looking to buy an airplane as complex as a Turbo Lance, I would try to work with the owner to get him to pay for any major repairs, while I paid for a fresh annual at time of purchase. If financing is involved, the path from the prior owner to you, via an annual where all the repairs are paid for before the airplane changes hands, can get very convoluted. It's all for the best if all parties work out all the details prior to pulling inspection plates, so that no one gets surprised. I hate surprises when it comes to airplanes—especially when I'm in the middle of a purchase.

If you have a family, and are looking for a high performance single-engine airplane, you should take a look at the Turbo Lance. Only 415 were built during the two years (1978–1979) the Turbo Lance was in production, so they don't show too regularly on the pre-owned aircraft market. A zero-time engine, aftermarket intercooler, Collins radios, and a lot of other equipment, including oxygen on a Turbo Lance with 2,300hr TT will set you back $73,000. When compared to a newer Turbo Saratoga, the plane that replaced the Lance, selling at $130,000, the Lance begins to look good. As for the matter of the T-tail and its idiosyncrasies, the best way for you to settle the matter to your satisfaction, is to go fly

Turbo Lance II Specifications

Engine: Lycoming TIO-540-S1AD, 300hp, 1,800hr TBO
Maximum Weight: 3,600lb
Fuel Capacity: 98gal
Maximum Speed: 193mph
Cruise Speed: 175kt
Fuel Consumption: 18.8gph
Range: 678nm
Rate of Climb at Sea Level: 1,000fpm
Service Ceiling: 20,000ft
Takeoff Ground Run: 960ft
Takeoff over 50ft Obstacle: 1,660ft
Landing Ground Roll: 880ft
Landing over 50ft Obstacle: 1,710ft
Stall Speed: 70kt
Standard Empty Weight: 2,071lb
Maximum Useful Load: 1,529lb
Wing Span: 32.8ft
Length: 28.9ft
Height: 9.5ft

The Turbo Lance II's cruise speed increased to 175kt, and with the fuel topped off at 98gal, you can keep one aloft for about 680nm before returning to earth. With performance like this, and the aircraft's 20,000ft ceiling, most trips can now be non-stop and often above the weather. For some users the result can be greater economy despite the bigger sticker price up front. That sticker price, at this writing, runs from $60,000 to about $80,000 for all variants of the Lance model.

some different six-place airplanes, and see for yourself how they compare to a T-tail.

Saratoga and Turbo Saratoga SP

In 1980, Piper decided to quit producing the Cherokee Six and the Lance. The new airplane to replace both was the PA-32 Saratoga and Turbo Saratoga SP. The straight-leg Saratoga was discontinued in 1990, the retractable Turbo SP was last built in 1991. Piper has returned the Saratoga to production in 1993 with the Saratoga IIhp. It's being built as a turbocharged 300hp retractable only, the fixed-gear Saratoga still out of production.

Piper's original intent with the Saratoga was to build a six-place single that could be had either as a fixed-gear, normally-aspirated single (although a few were built with turbocharging) or as a retractable turbocharged, 300hp airplane capable of operating at 25,000ft. Both airplanes featured club seating where the second two seats were turned rearwards with the idea of providing a business-type arrangement for the passengers in the back. To me, it always seemed like the space was not quite big enough for eight legs to find a place to stretch out unless the passengers played even-odd with their feet. Also, sitting in a small plane and facing where we had been, was a strange sensation. Most of the time, if only four were flying, people in the second row kept turning around to see what was happening up front. Sometimes, one of the rear passengers would sit in the last row of seats, leaving the middle passenger more room to look around.

The Saratoga's biggest advancements over the Lance were the return to a conventional tail and the use of the Warrior tapered wing. The Turbo does make for a stable plat-

> **Saratoga and Turbo Saratoga Rating**
> Investment: #1
> Utility: #1
> Popularity: #1+ (I want one)

form to take four people on a long cross-country. Most of the SPs have been fitted with built-in oxygen for all seats. Plan a high altitude flight, fill the tanks, plug in your oxygen mask, and go.

We flew San Jose to Seattle a couple of months ago in a Saratoga SP. For a number of reasons, I elected to stay below 18,000ft for the duration of the trip. Partially because I might have to make two unplanned stops along the way and didn't want to have to chop up my flight plan, and partially to be able to deviate to see the scenery.

We elected to go on oxygen and climb until we saw the best groundspeed. Passing through 15,000ft, the loran began showing an increase in groundspeed from 160kt upward. We leveled out at 16,500 when the loran showed 177kt over the ground. We were flying a course of 345deg for most of the trip so we had to stay at 16,500ft or go IFR to climb to an assigned altitude. Where we were was low enough for the first-time passengers to compare the countryside with the #CF-16 World

Aeronautical Chart (WAC) that we were using. Two of them were rather queasy about flying in an airplane of any kind, to say nothing of a small single, so I kept them busy helping me "navigate" the airplane. They soon figured out how to read the chart and plot our progress for the duration of the flight. As the airplane was being helped along by a Century 41 autopilot, I had the time to work with them during the flight. I figured the time was well spent kindling an interest in aviation. One passenger said at the end of the flight that if she had known it was "so fascinating and so much fun to fly little airplanes, I would have flown years ago." Well, that was all to the positive and it saved the sick-sacks from use—a good time was had by all.

With the power set to 65 percent we were able to cover the distance in 3.5hr. Average speed on the loran was 173kt. Best economy range for the Turbo Saratoga at that power setting is 23.9in of manifold pressure (MP) and 2,400rpm, a speed of 156kt at 16,000ft. We

The basic, plain vanilla Saratoga was sold from 1980 until 1990 and was introduced as a replacement for the Cherokee Six and the Lance. The Saratoga was offered in "straight leg" and retractable models; the fixed gear model is now out of production, but the retractable is (at this writing) being built again after a dry spell that lasted from 1991 to 1993. It is, like its predecessor, a six-place single.

Piper returned to the conventional tail layout with the Saratoga after flirting with the trendy T-tail on the Lance. The fixed gear Saratoga, posing coyly for the camera here, trades 20mph in airspeed for lower acquisition and maintenance costs.

This 1980 fixed gear Saratoga, if on the market today, will sell for about 85 percent of its original value—anywhere from $90,000 to $140,000 at current market values. The Saratoga was an outgrowth of the Cherokee Six/Lance with the new tapered wing and straight tail. It was offered in both fixed and retractable, turbocharged and normally aspirated versions. The Saratoga SP, also introduced in 1980, could be differentiated by the large oval air intake below the spinner.

were holding between 174 and 177kt for the entire portion of the flight at 16,500, gaining 20kt from the tailwind.

For those of you who haven't flown something with the capabilities of a 300hp turbocharged engine, here's something to ponder. How far from the destination airport would you have to start letting down from 16,500ft to a runway at 500ft elevation? Figuring a standard descent rate of 500fpm for 16,000ft gives you 32min to drop to the runway elevation. Thirty-two minutes at 170kt per hour is a distance of 88nm. To keep from blowing into the traffic area at 170kt, you had better plan to either start your descent farther out, increase the rate of descent, or plan on slowing down the airplane while a ways out. Now, I'm like most of you, I fly a Saratoga SP for speed. I don't plan on flying to 100nm from the airport and pulling the power back to 100kt to lose altitude. The turbo wouldn't appreciate the shock cooling, for one thing, and I was paying $150 per hour to fly the airplane, for another. Getting on the ground within the shortest time was my intention. I notified Flight Following, at that time Portland Center, that I would be beginning a descent about 20 miles north of their city, 75nm from our destination. I elected to keep the airspeed as high as possible during the descent, only slowing when I was within 10 miles of

the airport. This gave me 70 miles to come down to pattern altitude of 1,500ft with 105kt as a downwind speed. Seventy miles sounds like a long distance to cover coming down, but it was less than 20min at my present speed.

As we started down, I pulled 1in of manifold pressure for every 2,000ft of altitude in order to keep the engine warm throughout the descent. If I saw that we would still be high as we approached the airport, I could have dropped the gear at 132kt to help us down. As we slowed to the white arc on the airspeed indicator, the first 10deg of flaps could come in. This would be a good time to have the speed brake option.

All the passengers enjoyed the flight. They even said they might fly with me again someday. As I was their way back home, I didn't take their comments too seriously.

The visit went well. Three days later we were off for the return. Some of Seattle's famous weather was beginning to show up, so rather than go up high where the clouds were building, most of the flight home was spent below 10,000ft. We even had time to go fly through the crater made when Mt. St. Helens blew its top May 18, 1980. Flying over the crown, down into the still-smoking fire pit, out the north side and over the vast miles of downed trees was one of the strangest flights I have ever made. When directly over the lava dome in the crater, we could smell the sulfur dioxide steaming from a fissure 1,000ft below.

The fixed-gear Saratoga gives up 20mph to the retractable, according to the book. What you do gain, is the freedom from gear-related problems and their cost. Just like the Cherokee Six, the Saratoga makes a good load hauler. The fixed-gear weighs 100lb less than its retractable relation, and this is reflected in the useful load. Either airplane can carry almost 1,000lb, with a 102gal load of fuel, over 700nm. Both airplanes can be equipped with a three-bladed prop as an option. Where the three-blade shows an improvement over the standard two-blade prop is on the takeoff.

The three-blade cuts 170ft off the takeoff run and 186ft off the distance over a 50ft obstacle. Worth having if you work out of short strips with a heavy load. Also, the three-blade offers more ground clearance and quieter operation.

The two Saratogas are almost dimensionally the same, with the Turbo SP a little longer due to its large air intake below the prop.

Recent sales of both models show the Saratoga, whatever the guise, holding their

"Jeeze, we'll never get all this stuff in there!" the guy seems to be saying, but the Saratoga's double doors and up to 1,629lb useful load can accommodate for a lot of stuff. With full fuel (102gal) you can still haul almost 1,000lb into the sky and deliver it to someplace over 700nm away.

Saratoga and Turbo Saratoga Specifications

Engine:
301—Lycoming IO-540-K1G5, 300hp, 2,000hr TBO
301T—Lycoming TIO-540-S1AD, 300hp, 1,800hr TBO
Maximum Weight: 3,600lb
Fuel Capacity: 102gal
Maximum Speed:
301—175mph
301T—205mph
Cruise Speed:
301—172mph
301T—190mph
Fuel Consumption at 75% Power:
301—18gph
301T—19.9gph
Range at 75% Power:
301—784nm
301T—730nm
Rate of Climb at Sea Level:
301—990fpm
301T—1,075fpm
Service Ceiling:
301—14,100ft
301T—20,000ft
Takeoff Ground Run:
301—1,183ft
301T—1,110ft
Takeoff over 50ft Obstacle:
301—1,759ft
301T—1,590ft
Landing over 50ft Obstacle:
301—1,612ft
301T—1,725ft
Landing Ground Roll: 732ft
Stall Speed: 67mph
Standard Empty Weight:
301—1,986lb
301T—2,073lb
Maximum Useful Load:
301—1,629lb
301T—1,544lb
Wing Span: 36ft 2in
Length:
301—27ft 8 in
301T—28ft 2in
Height: 8ft 2 in

Saratoga SPs, like this one, have never been cheap, and this one probably went out the door for about $110,000 when new. It is worth nearly that today. A new SP IIhp, though, will have a sticker price of $310,000 and for the right owner, that will be a good investment.

value at almost 85 percent of their retail price when new. Average prices for a 1983 fixed-gear, in excellent condition, with 1,600hr TT, 100hr SMOH, is $130,000. It went out the door for $155,000 in 1983 and now still holds value well at 84 percent of new. A 1988 SP will sell

The three bladed prop was offered as an option on both the fixed and retractable gear models of the Saratoga; it is most effective during takeoff, where it reduces the run by 170ft and the distance over a 50ft obstacle by 186ft.

The Saratogas, of all types, are extremely popular and desirable. They are quite utilitarian and, according to many in the market, an excellent investment relative to the competition.

for $173,000 and a new SP IIhp has a sticker of $310,000. Expect to pay the full retail value for any Saratoga, as the owners know what the airplane is worth and that nothing else in the price range has the load-carrying capability of the big single. In 1988 a Saratoga SP with full King IFR radios, oxygen, intercom, HSI, but without air conditioning went for $205,000. Today it's 50 percent higher. The big jump in price can partially be explained by inflation, but according to the August 1993 *AOPA Pilot*, the managing practices of Piper, five years ago, didn't make for much, if any, profit; partially contributing to the company's financial problems and bankruptcy in 1991. At that time Piper was down to enough money for a good lunch at McDonald's. They seem to be on a rebound—I hope they sell lots of new airplanes.

Chapter 6

The Teaching Indian

Tomahawk

The PA-38 Tomahawk was to be Piper's answer to a basic training aircraft to replace the Cessna 152, a tough spot to fill. Piper's idea was to build a trainer that could run toe-to-toe with Cessna without the extra cost incurred with a Warrior. At the time of introduction in 1978, a Cessna 152 cost $20,075, a Warrior $30,605, and a Tomahawk could be picked up for $21,470, a good $10,000 under the Warrior

and close to the 152 when both were equipped with similar avionics. That's one of the reasons that Piper offered a special avionics group. If all T-hawks were built to the same specification, with the same option package, then costs could be kept in line with the Cessna 152. The Special Training Package from Piper included:

Night Lighting
Advance Instrument Package

The PA-38 Tomahawk is a stark, simple little trainer that was introduced in 1978 and sold extremely well—over a thousand in just the first year—partly because they cost $10,000 less than a Warrior. With a cruise speed of 118mph (claimed) and a wing-mounted, wide-track landing gear and semi-T-tail, the PA-38 keeps fledgling pilots from getting into too much trouble. With that cruise speed, it keeps anyone from straying too far from home on a weekend afternoon, too. They are still the simple, economical introduction to flying they were intended to be and are available at just about every airport in the country, in just about every condition imaginable.

Aircraft Tow Bar
True Airspeed Indicator
Entrance Step—Left and Right
Dual Toe Brakes
Sun Visors
Tinted Windshield and Windows
Avionics:
King KX-170B 720 Channel Transceiver,
200 Channel Nav Receiver with Antennas
King KI-208 Indicator with VOR/Loc
Converter
Telex 66C Microphone
Telex 600 Ohm Headset
Poly Planar Cabin Speaker

Piper wanted to capture more of the primary trainer market than they were getting with the more expensive Warrior. Also, the Warrior was a lot more airplane than the Tomahawk or 152 and required more effort to learn to fly. The T-hawk wasn't burdened with dragging two extra seats around with the resultant higher fuel burn and heavier airplane. Loaded with one nervous student and one long-suffering instructor, the T-hawk weighed in at a sultry 1,670lb compared to the Warrior at 2,325lb. The fuel burn with 112hp was considerably less than with the Warrior's 160hp. Students aren't really in any hurry to go anywhere. Building time and learning maneuvers at 100kt is much more important than burning a hole through the sky at 127kt in the bigger airplane.

Piper designed the T-hawk with the instructor in mind. A questionnaire was sent out to over 10,000 flight instructors asking what they would want most in a training aircraft. The answers came back and Piper read them carefully. Good visibility, sturdy landing gear, economy of operation, and a quiet cabin were all qualities important to good flight instruction.

Two doors, instead of the Warrior's one, headed the list of requirements. Perhaps the

instructors wanted the option of departing the airplane when the student did something other than fly in the proper manner, but I think it was more for ease of entry and exit than anything else.

If you are in the market for a Tomahawk for purposes other than a flight school, such as an inexpensive way to build time, a couple of points to consider before buying one. First point: Piper pushed the last ones out the door in 1982, then offered "Cadets," built on the Warrior airframe, when they began building trainers again in 1988. Five years and just under 2,500 built isn't a very long run for an airplane that was supposed to replace all the Cessna 152s at the flight schools. Cessna quit building 152s in 1985, along with most of their piston-engine airplanes; however, there are still quite a few Cessna 152s trundling students through the sky and the older ones just keep getting remanufactured or rebuilt for FBOs to use as trainers, while the Tomahawks keep fading into the background.

Second point: almost all the Tomahawks for sale have been used as trainers, amassing lots of student hours on the airframes. It isn't all that uncommon to see 4,000–7,000hr TT on the listed airplanes. If you remember your first twenty or so hours in a primary trainer, you have a good idea as to how these airplanes have been flown for much of their life. Not that high airframe time is all that bad, mind you. It's just that a Tomahawk that has spent the majority of its time flying patterns and going thud on the runway bears careful checking out prior to money changing hands.

Most people don't return to primary trainers when buying an aircraft for personal use, nevertheless there are a few scenarios where I could see a T-hawk filling an owner's need. If you are looking for a way to get off the ground all by yourself, or with a small co-pilot and you don't foresee anyone else flying with you in the future, then perhaps a Tomahawk will fit you well. Or, if financial considerations limit you to an under $10,000 airplane and you would rather purchase a newer two-place than a four-seater that has seen 20 years of problems, then a T-hawk might be the right airplane for you.

Take your time when shopping for a Tomahawk. Find one with less than 1,500hr

Tomahawk Rating
Utility: #2
Popularity: #4
Investment: #5 (No money to be made, just lost)

TT that never earned its keep as a trainer. Hard to do, harder to find, but well worth the effort. If you limit yourself to low-time airplanes, on their first engine, then you could come up with a nice, fairly new, low-cost method of flying. Look for all the other problems that come with used aircraft: corrosion, landing damage, metal shavings in the oil, anything out of line in the logs—that sort of thing.

I found one that had spent its entire life in a hangar; it looked like it just came in on its maiden ferry flight from Lock Haven. The tach showed only 1,410hr TT. It had recently completed an extensive annual with no major squawks. The logs were very boring, nothing other than annuals and oil changes for the most part. That's the kind we like to see. Surprisingly enough, the owner wasn't asking any more for her airplane than some others with high airframe time. This one would be the Tomahawk to pick, if you are looking for a good one. Clean, low-time, corrosion-free Tomahawks do come up on the market from time to time. Just like anything else in demand, they go quickly. Take some time to learn what makes one tick. Go walk a few airport flight lines. Get a feel for what a Tomahawk in good condition looks like. Go offer an owner some gas money in exchange for a ride. Tomahawk owners are pretty much like all the other general aviation owners, they like

Tomahawks are currently available very cheaply, sometimes for well under $10,000. That's because it is a small, noisy, tight little cockpit designed for two small occupants maximum. The T-tail's handling qualities are not favored by a lot of pilots who've flown the airplane, but others consider it just fine. There are ten in the current *Trade-A-Plane*, ranging in price from $7,000 to $17,000.

to talk. For the investment of a couple of hours of fuel, about 10gal, you will receive an education that can't be found in books.

Tomahawk Typical Specifications

Engine: Lycoming O-235-L2C, 112hp, 2,000hr TBO
Maximum Weight: 1,670lb
Fuel Capacity: 32gal
Maximum Speed at Sea Level: 109kt
Cruise Speed: 109kt at 75% power at 7,500ft
Range: 452nm at 75% power (45min reserve); 640nm at 55% power (no reserve)
Rate of Climb: 718fpm
Service Ceiling: 12,000ft
Takeoff Ground Run: 975ft
Takeoff Over 50ft Obstacle: 1,400ft
Landing Ground Roll: 595ft
Landing Over 50ft Obstacle: 1,465ft
Stall Speed: 46kt (flaps extended)
Standard Empty Weight: 1,088lb
Maximum Useful Load: 582lb
Wing Span: 34ft
Length: 23.1ft

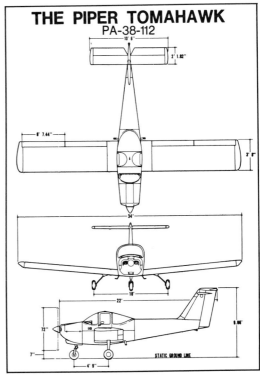

The Tomahawk was designed to offer good visibility for the student and the instructor.

The Bigger Indians

Seminole and Turbo Seminole

The Seminole is Piper's entry into the light twin, multi-engine trainer market. It was built from 1979 to 1982, and by special order in some following years. The Seminole is very much like an Archer with two 180hp engines instead of one. The cabin seats four, with a baggage compartment behind the seats. A full load of fuel weighs 648lb. Figuring another 100lb off the useful load for avionics, this leaves 646lb for people and baggage. Four FAA-standard 170lb people come to 680lb, so

A lot of PA-44 Seminoles have been built and are in use, often as a cheap multi-engine trainer. It seats four and will cruise at 192mph. A turbocharged, pressurized version with 20,000ft ceiling is available, at a price. The Seminole was first introduced in 1979. The Turbo came along in 1981. Both were offered until production ceased in 1982. Rumor has it that Piper will build you a new one if you send them enough money.

The Seminole is a kind of "Twin Archer." It is a good choice for someone who wants twin-engine reliability for IFR or night flying. Its service ceiling is rated at 17,100ft for the standard version, but those are "factory feet," and in the author's experience you can plan on about 14,000ft.

if you want to carry people and a reasonable 200lb load of suitcases and other baggage, some fuel has to be left behind.

The Seminole works well for someone flying with one other person, who wants the reliability of two engines for IFR or night flying. The service ceiling is listed at 17,100ft, but the airplane is all out of chuff at 14,000. Plan your flights to stay below 10,000ft and you'll have no problems. Piper built a few Turbo Seminoles, capable of reaching much higher. If you consistently need to go higher than 10,000ft, you should get one of the Turbo Seminoles.

Myself and two others were flying a non-turbo Seminole out of Bishop, California, trying to cross the Sierra Nevadas on our way to home-port San Jose. We were chasing cloud tops building over the mountains

One of the virtues of the Seminole is that it is quite comfortable for a light twin; you can fly longer distances in greater comfort than in many other airplanes. Shown is a 1981 Turbo Seminole.

Seminoles are currently priced anywhere from about $55,000 on up to $300,000, and there are comparatively few to choose from. Since it was built for only about three years, there are not a lot of parts around—a consideration to factor into a buying decision.

while a storm was moving in to the area from behind us.

Bishop is located on the San Francisco Sectional Chart, 2 miles off Highway 395 on the eastern side of the Sierras. It's at 4,120ft elevation, giving us a head start in our climb to an 11,500ft cruise altitude, needed to clear the tops of the rocks. The only problem was, the clouds were climbing faster than we were. I finally gave up flying in circles when we were at 14,000ft, with only 150fpm rate of climb.

A turn to the south, along with a gradual descent let us fly down the Owens Valley until a turn to 270deg put us in line with Visalia, California. The mountains were between 8,000ft to 12,123ft in that area, however a pass at 7,000ft made crossing easier. We had left the clouds behind us 15min ago, and all the sky around us showed clear, including the pass. The owner of the airplane said it was time to make the airplane go, as he wanted to get home soon, so I put the nose over while shoving the throttles forward.

We had left Las Vegas in the morning, playing touch-tag with the weather all the way. He bought the gas and made the decisions, so it was time to go! Visalia to San Jose is normally a 1hr 10min flight at 160kt cruise speeds. We smoked into the San Jose area in less than 55min. Everything firewalled, the Apollo 50 loran showed 177kt groundspeed. It helped that we could use the altitude difference between our present 10,500ft and pattern altitude of 1,100ft to keep speed up on the way home. Part of the speed was gained by holding a 200–300fpm descent for some of the flight. That's when I began to enjoy turbocharged airplanes a little more.

The turbocharged Seminole was manufactured only in 1981 and 1982, and only 86 airplanes were manufactured The early ones, similar to the one I was flying, were non-turbocharged with a ceiling to prove it. The turbo has a maximum certified altitude of 20,000ft which would have let us make the trip over the mountains with altitude to spare. Also, our time to altitude would have been cut significantly, making for a shorter stay up high.

The Seminole we brought back to San Jose spent most of its time as a multi-engine trainer, a job it does willingly. If I lived where the ground stayed flat and level like it belongs, then a Seminole would make for a good cross-country instrument platform with the safety of twin engines. The airplane in the story above, had been bought in Memphis to

---

Seminole and Turbo Seminole Specifications

Engines:
Seminole—Lycoming O-360-E1A6D, 180hp, 2,000hr TBO
Turbo—Lycoming L/TO-360-E1A6D, 180hp 1,800hr TBO
Maximum Weight:
Seminole—3,800lb
Turbo—3,943lb
Fuel Capacity: 108gal
Maximum Speed:
Seminole—166kt
Turbo—195kt
Cruise Speed:
Seminole—159kt
Turbo—183kt
Fuel Consumption: 21gph
Range:
Seminole—915nm at 159kt (45min reserve)
Turbo—820nm at 183kt (45min reserve)
Rate of Climb at Sea Level:
Seminole—1,340fpm
Turbo—1,290fpm
Service Ceiling:
Seminole—17,100ft
Turbo—20,000ft
Takeoff Ground Run: 880ft
Takeoff over 50ft Obstacle: 1,400ft
Landing Ground Roll: 590ft
Landing over 50ft Obstacle: 1,400ft
Stall Speed: 54kt
Standard Empty Weight:
Seminole—2,406lb
Turbo—2,461lb
Maximum Useful Load:
Seminole—1,394lb
Turbo—1,482lb
Wing Span: 40ft 7in
Length: 34ft 5in
Height: 13ft 3in
Seats: 4

be ferried to its new home in San Jose. I was to fly it home with the owner and another pilot on board. We stopped at Wichita Falls, Texas, for the first refuel. Next, on to Albuquerque, New Mexico. Then to Las Vegas, Nevada, for the night.

I consider an airplane comfortable if I don't have to be helped out after 5hr in the left seat. We covered more than 10hr in the Seminole in the first day and I was still ambulatory at the end of the flight.

Because the plane was only built for three years, it is not a very common airplane on the used market. Parts are getting quite hard to locate, with a premium charged for anything that can be found.

The book shows a value $76,000 for a 1980, but I was able to locate one in the middle $50,000 range, with 4,500hr TT and mid-time engines. Occasionally a Seminole can be found that Piper built to order during the nineties. They turn up from time to time in the $300,000 range. Lately there is a 1993 for sale in *Trade-A-Plane* as a factory demo for "only" $299,000. Rush right out.

Like any other airplane, have a Seminole checked by the experts. Especially as most of the airplanes saw a multitude of pilots behind the yokes as multi-engine trainers. Before laying down $70,000 for a 1978, find out whether replacement parts are available, such as landing gear struts (they crack after a lot of landings). It's rather expensive to have your airplane sit in a hangar waiting for nonexistent parts to arrive. There were only 469 built of both models. Attrition has burned up its share and what's left wears out the same parts as yours, so finding much of anything in a salvage yard will be next to impossible.

Apache

The PA-23 Apache was the first Piper with an Indian name. It was introduced in 1954 as Piper's original light twin and its first airplane aimed specifically at the executive transport market. Driven by two Lycoming

The PA-23 Apache is starting to look something like a relic, or maybe a collector's airplane, but there are still a lot of them around and many even fly. It looks old fashioned, and is. The PA-23 was built from 1954 to 1960 as an economical light twin. It has an alleged cruise of 150mph. They are very common in California, and with just about the lowest sticker price of any twin on the lot. Some owners buy them as inexpensive multi-engine time builders while others like their antique design. The Apache has the now-novel feature of a landing gear that still works even with the wheels up, since the wheels are still exposed when retracted. The idea was that you could save the airframe even if the gear failed to drop—a problem more common in the Apache's design era than today.

150hp engines, it was a rather poor single-engine performer until the power was increased in 1962 to 235hp per side, improving its single-engine rate of climb from not very much to 220fpm. Maximum cruise speed was upped to 191mph, a major improvement over the original 170mph.

The Apache is a solid, four-place, retractable twin that was Piper's flagship during the late fifties. A new version with 250hp engines, the Aztec, was introduced in 1960. Both the Aztec and Apache carried the same PA-23 designation, and the Apache soldiered on alongside the Aztec until the Apache was discontinued in 1963. During the last few years of Apache production, its biggest competition was from other Piper twins, namely the Aztec and Twin Comanche. Piper finally saw that sales of the more modern twins were being hurt by Apache sales, so the company dropped the Apache from production.

Apache Typical Specifications
Engines:
1954—Lycoming O-320, 150hp, 2,000hr TBO
1962—Lycoming O-540, 235hp, 2,000hr TBO
Maximum Weight:
1954—3,500lb
1963—4,800lb
Fuel Capacity: 108gal (standard); 144gal (optional)
Cruise Speed: 170mph (150hp engines); 191mph (235hp engines)
Range: 1,250 miles
Rate of Climb at Sea Level: 1,350fpm
Single Engine Rate of Climb: 220fpm at 4,800lb (235hp engines)
Service Ceiling: 20,000ft
Takeoff Ground Run: 900ft
Takeoff over 50ft Obstacle: 1,600ft
Landing Ground Roll: 880ft
Landing over 50ft Obstacle: 1,360ft
Stall Speed: 62mph
Maximum Useful Load: 1,320lb
Seats: 4 (5-seat option)

Over the last forty years, the Apache has gone from a luxurious mode of travel to an inexpensive trainer logging hours with a student behind the yoke. Most of the Apaches still flying are being used as semi-inexpensive multi-engine time builders by pilots on their way to an aviation job. Because of its low resale value, the 150hp model is usually flown to TBO, or beyond, then rebuilt with larger engines or parted out.

Not only was the Apache burdened with low performance, but also it failed badly in the looks department when compared to the Aztec or Twin Comanche (introduced in 1963). As with all the other older Piper twins, many modifications have been incorporated into the Apache over its 40-year life span. The biggest visual change is the "long nose" conversion. Initially advertised as a speed improvement, the nose change probably is aimed more at the eyeball than at the airspeed indicator.

One good attribute is the Apache's load-carrying capacity. If all but the pilot's seat are pulled, more than 2,000lb can be loaded on board the 235hp model—largest payload for any four-place light twin of its time. It still looks like a flying potato, though, but a sturdy one at that. As with the other fifties-era designs, the Apache is built with a "standard bridge construction" airframe similar to what most manufacturers were using on their early multi-engine airplanes, so it will be around for quite some time to come.

Most of the PA-23s have had their avionics panels overhauled at least once since their initial tube type, 90- or 320-channel, radios were installed at the factory. A lot of the value of the airplane will be determined by the type of avionics retrofitted.

If you find one with the original crystal-controlled Narco VHF Nav/Coms installed, best figure on turning them into museum pieces and install some modern avionics—something in the King KX-170 or Narco MK-12D would be a good start.

Time left on the engines will be the other most important factor in determining price. An overhaul on the Lycoming 540s will set you back $15,000 per side, prop rebuild extra. The average resale of a vintage Apache is under $25,000, making the cost of the engines a major determining factor. A few Apaches are being offered for sale with engines that haven't been apart in a very long time—beware. Just being low- or mid-time isn't enough to go by. Lycoming puts a time span on their TBOs, as well as an hour limit. If nothing else, I'd want to borescope and run an oil analysis on any motor that's been operating over ten years just to be sure that all is right inside. There is a possibility that the airplane has been sitting on a ramp for many years, doing nothing but rusting, wearing out without moving.

I have had the sorry experience, in the past, of buying low-time instead of condition. The airplane only had 760hr on the engine, less than 2,300hr on the airframe, and it looked good on the outside. Turns out that it had spent a lot of time tied down instead of flying. By the time I had accumulated 50hr, the oil consumption was running over one quart per hour, a bit more than acceptable. Turns out that the prop had sat in one position so long that the piston rings rusted to the cylinder walls. When the airplane was fired up about 2hr prior to my purchase, the rust on the rings scored the cylinders badly. The damage didn't show up for the first few hours of operation until the engine had been run enough to really get some serious wear.

Seven thousand dollars, six new cylinders, and a few $55 exhaust valves later, the oil consumption dropped to less than one quart per 15hr. I learned an expensive lesson. The cost to run the airplane so far had worked out to $140 per hour for maintenance alone. As I have stressed before, if you don't know more about the airplane than the people who work on it, spend the time and money to have a competent shop check it over very carefully. Remember, the airplane of your dreams hasn't been manufactured for 30-some years; think carefully about buying something that can turn into a money pit.

Aztec and Turbo Aztec

The PA-23 Aztec was an end product of all the Apache's seating, power, airframe, and performance changes, and was built from the same fuselage as the Apache. Except for the Aztec's larger 250hp engines, different paint scheme, and longer nose, the Aztec and

The Aztec replaced the Apache, beginning in 1960. It seats six, cruises about 50mph faster at about 204mph, and was built in many variations. These variants have noses that have progressively gotten longer, somewhat like Pinocchio's, perhaps for exaggerating cruise speed or range data. It is available with turbocharged engines.

Apache were nearly identical. The Aztec remained in production from 1960 to 1981. A turbocharged Aztec, the PA-23T, was introduced in 1966 and it remained in production through 1981.

As the two decades plus of the Aztec's life went by, numerous changes were made to every part of the airplane except the main airframe. Along with the standard airplane, a turbocharged version was offered in 1966 as the Turbo C. Prior to this, Rajay turbos were approved as an aftermarket installation on the standard 250hp Aztec from 1960 until the introduction of Piper's own puffer model. Any one of the turbo-powered planes will cruise along at the lower flight levels with 200kt on the airspeed indicator for what seems like forever.

The Aztec is a large, comfortable airplane with four on board, the fifth and sixth seats being for real good friends or children. An 800nm trip with standard tanks goes by in

Aztec and Turbo Aztec Rating
Investment: #3
Utility: #2
Popularity: #2

In its day the Aztec was one of the most popular, best selling twins in the world. And it is still much in demand, commanding prices approximately double those of Apaches. Current *Trade-A-Plane* prices range from $41,000 to $120,000. With an Apache you can drone around the sky, building multi-engine time without actually leaving the neighborhood. With the Aztec's 210mph normal cruise and 1,300 miles range (with tip tanks), you and your friends can go places and do things.

less than 4.5hr. Tip tanks added, the range, with 45min reserves, moves out to over 1,100 miles.

The later Turbo Fs were set up with automatic waste gate controllers to prevent overboost at full throttle, and a differential pressure controller that provides constant manifold pressure during climb and descent. However, the earlier Rajay installations had to be monitored at all times to prevent kicking the manifold pressure over the red line, doing drastic things to the TBO. This is a little harder than it would first appear. When the first two-thirds of the throttle is applied, not a whole lot happens other than noise. It takes a couple of seconds for the blowers to come up to their 120,000rpm operating speed, as the exhaust flow has to get running before it can spin up the impellers and make positive boost. When the boost goes up, the fun really begins. First, you get the shove in the back as

The Aztec F was delivered with 250hp Lycomings starting in 1971, with or without turbo. New wing tip tanks (shown) add 40gal and 300 miles range to the earliest models. Another feature of the F was the addition of improved fuel gauges and anti-slosh baffles in the fuel cells for more accurate readings.

the horsepower goes from under 100 to 250 in seconds. Then you get to chase the manifold pressure needle all over the gauge while it lifts past overboost.

See—it doesn't take full throttle at sea level to make a turbocharged engine produce full rated power. You need almost full throttle to make the power start to climb, then as it comes on, a fast reduction to come back into limits. Usual procedure is to bring in enough power to make the turbo go to work, then retard the throttle as the horsepower kicks in. Like running a racehorse: a fine touch with the reins is helpful. You develop the ability to stay within the limits or you get to replace a lot of very expensive bits and pieces.

The other method of controlling turbos is through a manually operated waste gate. This lets a portion of the exhaust gasses bypass the turbo's impeller section, limiting boost. By opening or closing the waste gate, the manifold pressure can be raised or lowered.

Big fun happens when trying to pull the power back to descend, drop the turbos off without shock-cooling the cylinders, enrich the mixture, talk to Approach Control, and fly the airplane. Kind of a dance for four hands. It helps a lot if you have everything figured out in advance, because if you get behind the airplane, you're liable to find yourself on a longer cross-country than intended. Or end up on short final with 120kt airspeed, and you know how hard the brakes will have to work

The Aztec E's landing light was flush mounted—a real selling point, apparently, for this young lady in a 1970 factory photo.

to haul down the airplane from that speed—especially on a 3,000ft runway.

All humor aside, if a Turbo Aztec is the airplane of your dreams, perhaps it would be better to look for a model built after the turbocharger became standard, say a 1970 Turbo D. Then all you have to watch is the throttle; all the turbo controls are automatic.

The later airplanes usually sold with 177gal long-range fuel capacity, picked up by the additional two tip tanks of 20gal capacity each. The optional tanks interconnect with the outboard mains, keeping fuel management simplified on long flights.

All members of the Aztec tribe came with fuel injection. The Aztec F claimed the highest useful load capacity in its class: 2,012lb for the turbo version and 2,151lb for the normally aspirated engine.

You could fit four sets of golf clubs in that nose, or maybe a corpse, or anything else that would fit and that wouldn't tilt the CG out of limits. The Aztec E airframe will carry a 2,000lb (alleged) useful load, part of which may be six people. The factory says they will be seated in plush comfort. There were 2,472 Aztecs delivered to customers during the sixties alone.

Going up high to 21,000ft, a pilot friend of mine picked up a 110kt tailwind and really skipped along on a flight to Memphis in his old blender. He said the loran showed a groundspeed in the 300kt per hour range, making a 490nm trip in less than two and a half hours from ramp to ramp.

The nose compartment holds 150lb of baggage in 21cu-ft, leaving the cabin free for passengers' feet. The aft storage area is usually somewhat filled with an oxygen bottle, but there is still enough room for the odd computer or two for use at the end of a business trip. The Aztec is really a great way to take four real-sized humans, and all the accouterments necessary to survive for two weeks, on a round-the-US vacation.

Or, you can put the Aztec to work, carrying two engineers and an architect out to a remote dirt runway at a construction site. Either way, the Aztec will fly missions that not many other airplanes can handle while still offering the room and comfort that the Aztec is known for.

An option list for the 1979 Turbo Aztec F reads like the Detroit Telephone Directory. All of the avionics usually were installed as a packaged unit. For $14,785 you got (hang on!): two Com radios, two VOR/Loc indicators

---

Aztec and Turbo Aztec Specifications

Engines:
23—Lycoming IO-540, 250hp, 2,000hr TBO
23T—Lycoming TIO-540-C1A, 250hp, 2,000hr TBO
Maximum Weight: 5,200lb
Fuel Capacity: 140gal (standard); 178gal (optional)
Maximum Speed:
23—179kt
23T—210kt
Cruise Speed:
23—179kt
23T—210kt
Fuel Consumption:
23—26gph
23T—33gph
Range:
23—790nm, 1,060nm (optional tanks)
23T—695nm, 945nm (optional tanks)
Rate of Climb at Sea Level:
23—1,400fpm
23T—1,470fpm
Service Ceiling:
23—17,600ft
23T—24,000ft
Takeoff Ground Run: 760ft
Takeoff over 50ft Obstacle: 990ft
Landing Ground Roll: 760ft
Landing over 50ft Obstacle: 1,585ft
Stall Speed: 54.5kt (flaps extended)
Standard Empty Weight:
23—3,221lb
23T—3,358lb
Maximum Useful Load:
23—1,979lb
23T—1,842lb
Wing Span: 37.3ft
Length: 31.2ft
Height: 10.1ft
Seats: 6

(one with glideslope), two VOR/Loc converters, glideslope receiver, ADF, transponder, audio panel, marker beacon light and receiver, autopilot, VOR/Loc coupling to autopilot, electric trim, microphone, headset, avionics master switch, power converters, and static discharge wicks. This is without adding color radar, DME, ARNAV, HSI, HF transceiver, intercom, map light, EGT gauge, and autopilot disconnect switch on the pilot's yoke. As hard as it might be to believe, all this was a very basic package. Things could go from this to a *really* complicated setup.

Avionics could be mixed and matched in such a way as to end up with a $40,000 pack-

An Aztec F in flight.

age in a $130,000 airplane. As time went on so did technology. Avionics and navigation equipment has changed drastically since the Aztec's inception. Now there is GPS, loran and radar altimeters to cope with, to mention but a few new navigation aids. Some of the older planes have had their panels completely made over, all new radios installed, up to $50,000 spent on making the older models fly and navigate like new.

A good early seventies Turbo E can be had for about $75,000. Newer ones can easily top $150,000, with a lot of the price dependent on what's in the panel and how many hours are on the engines. When looking at TBO, figure a minimum of $25,000 to pull and overhaul one engine and prop. That's if no other surprises pop up. Both engines done at the same time will eat up the better part of $50,000, probably closer to $65,000, props, pumps, and paint included. So you can see how a large part of the airplane price is wrapped up in engine time.

An old flounder flopping around the field with runout engines and an early sixties serial number shouldn't cost more than $30,000. If you are handy with a wrench and carry an A&P license, you might even get it to fly! The way new planes aren't being built, this might not be a bad expenditure. Find an older Aztec with a low-time airframe, rebuild it to new for less than $100,000, and come out

of the deal with an inexpensive (ha!) six-seat airplane. They're all built like bridges, so if the particular airplane you're interested in owning has less than 4,000hr TT, and the rust monster hasn't eaten the metal parts, you should be able to fly it well into the twenty-first century.

Twin Comanche, Twin Comanche C/R, and Turbo Twin Comanche C/R

First seen in 1963 as a sleek, high performance IFR platform, the PA-30 Twin Comanche was Piper's way of building a different airplane under the same type certificate as an existing airframe. The Twin Comanche was developed from the single-engine PA-24 Comanche, an airplane renowned for its aerodynamic efficiency. Other than a solid nose, two engines, and a higher rated load, it's the same airframe as the Comanche.

However, the twin-engine version underwent so many structural changes that it would be impossible to convert a PA-24 to this configuration. For example, even though

---

Twin Comanche Rating
Investment: #4
Utility: #3
Popularity: #3

---

the laminar wing of the Comanche was retained on the twin, heavier leading edges, skins, heavier wing root ribs, and heavier rear spar have been used in the PA-30's construction. Larger landing gear struts and heavier gear forgings are used. Even the baggage door and frame were redesigned for greater strength and construction simplicity.

The PA-30 sported two Lycoming 160hp engines and was built through 1969. In 1970, the PA-39 Twin Comanche and PA-39T Turbo Twin Comanche, propelled by two counter-rotating (C/R) Lycoming engines, were introduced. The Turbo's engines were of the same horsepower rating, but the Turbo was capable of operating in the low 20,000ft altitudes, cruising at 234mph for over 1,000 miles. Staying at 12,000ft only dropped the cruise to 221mph.

The early Twin Comanche engines, Lycoming IO-320s, were saddled with a 1,500hr TBO as late as 1966. A *Piper Pilot* in-house company paper for November 1966 advertised a Twin Comanche fitted with" ruggedized Lycomings, now approved for up to 1,500hr between overhauls." Fortunately this state of affairs no longer prevails—the IO-320 has turned out to be one of the most reliable airplane engines ever made. With proper care, it will easily make its 2,000hr TBO today.

Single-engine performance of the 1960s-era Twin Comanches wasn't too bad, considering the anemic climb rates of other light twins of that era. Ceiling was 7,000ft, reached at a single-engine rate of 260fpm. With both fans running, climb rate held at 1,460fpm from sea level. The turbo airplanes could maintain 1,100fpm at 10,000ft and fly at 12,600 on one engine.

In 1967 a few turbo models were made with deice capability. This gives them the capability of going flying in airspace where ice is reported. I'm not too sure I want to take a 26-year-old airplane with only 160hp per side through sky filled with hard pieces of water—I don't care how much deice capability it has. I find myself in the minority, though. Most owners have no problem with hard IFR flight.

The Twin Comanche was improved with counter-rotating propellers in 1970 and renamed the Twin Comanche C/R. On the original Twin Comanche, both engines spun in the same direction. Should the right engine fail, then the thrust from the left is inboard of the engine. Any tendency to yaw to the right is slight and can be countered by holding the

---

PA-39 and PA-39T Specifications

Engines:
PA-39—Lycoming L/IO-320-B1A, 160hp, 2,000hr TBO
PA-39T—Lycoming L/IO-320-C1A, 160hp, 1,800 TBO
Maximum Weight:
PA-39—3,600lb
PA-39T—3,725lb
Fuel Capacity:
PA-39—90gal
PA-39T—120gal
Maximum Speed:
PA-39—205mph
PA-39T—241mph
Cruise:
PA-39—198mph
PA-39T—221mph
Fuel Consumption:
PA-39—19.6gph
PA-39T—22.6gph
Range:
PA-39—830 miles
PA-39T—1,090 miles
Rate of Climb at Sea Level:
PA-39—1,460fpm
PA-39T—1,290fpm
Service Ceiling:
PA-39—20,000ft
PA-39T—25,000ft
Takeoff Ground Run:
PA-39—940ft
PA-39T—990ft
Takeoff over 50ft Obstacle:
PA-39—1,530ft
PA-39T—1,590ft
Landing Ground Roll:
PA-39—700ft
PA-39T—725ft
Landing over 50ft Obstacle:
PA-39—1,870ft
PA-39T—1,900ft
Stall Speed with Flaps: 70mph
Standard Empty Weight:
PA-39—2,270lb
PA-39T—2,416lb
Maximum Useful Load:
PA-39—1,330lb
PA-39T—1,309lb
Wing Span:
PA-39—36ft
PA-39T—36.8ft
Length: 25.2ft
Height: 8.2ft
Seats: 6 (4 on early models)

right wing up slightly and inputting a little left rudder. On the other hand, with only the right engine running, the thrust is outboard of the engine, increasing the tendency to yaw to the left and therefore requiring more right rudder and aileron, which raises drag and reduces the rate of climb. With the Twin Comanche C/R, the critical engine is eliminated. The thrust vector is now inboard on the right engine as well as on the left engine. Optimum single-engine directional control and performance is obtained on either engine.

If one of the fans quit, you were left with 160hp to carry a 3,600lb airplane. It wasn't so much a question of will it stay in the air, as how long will it fly before the ground reaches up to grab it. When the Twin Comanche grew into the PA-39 C/R with turbocharging, the airplane stood a better chance of flying on one engine.

For only having a total of 320hp, 40hp less than a Seminole's 360, the Twin Comanche will out-climb and out-run the Seminole at all power settings. The Seminole carries 200lb more weight than a Twin Comanche, but they almost have the same useful load. The Twin Comanche's airframe is cleaner than the Seminole's, partially accounting for the speed difference. In a similar manner, a Comanche 180 will blow the ailerons off a 180hp Archer. However, you get what you pay for when it comes to aerodynamics. The older airplanes are a much tighter fit. It's a cleaner airframe that gives it more go.

If you are flying a single-engine retractable and you want to buy a lot more performance while staying under $50,000, the price of a good, used 1981 Archer, looking at an older Twin Comanche might be a good idea. Going from the above-mentioned Archer to a 1965 Turbo Twin Comanche, at an advertised price of $57,000,will gain you a lot of go for your dough. Climb the Turbo Twin Comanche to 12,000ft, set the power to 2,400rpm and 28in of manifold pressure, and watch 220mph come up on the loran. Fuel burn will be 22.6gph, allowing a 1,000-mile range. Bring the airplane up to 20,000ft, and the speed climbs to 230mph with a 200-mile increase in range. Quite a jump from a 135mph Archer at 6,000ft, isn't it?

With all this performance comes a penalty. A two-decade-old, twin-engine, turbocharged airplane, showing 5,000hr TT, will definitely have its share of problems. At least 90 percent of unscheduled maintenance is due to the turbocharger. Everything is stressed harder when fitted with forced induction. Parts cook off the airplane with increasing regularity as the airframe ages. Even the unblown Twin Comanche is prone to maintenance hassles. Just the ADs on the airplanes are a merry lot. There's so many of them over the years that making sure of compliance at time of purchase is a big job.

Some of them, like AD #74-16-8, covering cracks in the aft bulkhead, have the possibility of being very expensive. AD #91-14-22 covers the Lycoming engine's crankshaft gears and alignment dowels. Especially if the airplane has landed gear-up, this AD becomes very important.

After any prop strike, the engines have to be opened and checked, but some owners just check for a bent crank and let it go at that. If the spec is within range, they put the prop back on and fly the airplane—only to blow a counterweight or crack a crank 200hr later, usually at the worst possible time.

Check any potential purchase very carefully. On a 25-year-old twin with turbos, check everything like your life depends on it. It does!

Seneca, Seneca II, and Seneca III

If you took a Cherokee Six, retracted the gear, hung engines on the wings, and fiberglassed the nose, you'd have the first PA-34 Seneca. Piper built the airplane with such straightforward flying characteristics that you can easily transition from a single to a multi-engine rating through a course of ten programmed steps at any Piper dealer. The Seneca, like some other Piper twins, has counter-rotating props designed to eliminate the "critical engine" factor.

The first Senecas, built from 1972 to 1974, were powered by the 180hp Lycoming IO-360s, probably the best aircraft engine made. The right side counter-rotating engine is designated LIO-360. Few of the LIO-360 engine parts will exchange with the IO-360 except cases and some other small parts. It takes a lot

There have been three basic versions of the popular PA-34 Seneca twin, models I, II, and III. The Seneca is essentially a Cherokee Six with an extra engine, 187mph cruise, and with accommodations for five or six. It's been a popular business and pleasure airplane, and there are lots of them to choose from. The Seneca was introduced in 1972 and grew into the Seneca III in 1976.

Seneca Rating
Investment: #1
Utility: #1
Popularity: #2

Seneca I Specifications
Engines: Lycoming L/IO-360-C1E6, 180hp, 2,000hr TBO
Maximum Weight: 4,000lb
Fuel Capacity: 100gal
Maximum Speed: 196kt
Cruise Speed: 173mph
Fuel Consumption: 20.6gph
Range: 861nm
Rate of Climb at Sea Level: 1,460fpm
Single Engine Rate of Climb: 190fpm
Service Ceiling: 18,800ft
Single Engine Service Ceiling: 3,650ft
Takeoff Ground Run: 800ft
Takeoff over 50ft Obstacle: 1,140ft
Landing Ground Roll: 705ft
Landing over 50ft Obstacle: 1,335ft
Stall Speed: 67mph (flaps extended)
Standard Empty Weight: 2,599lb
Maximum Useful Load: 1,601lb
Wing Span: 38.9ft
Length: 28.5ft
Height: 9.9ft
Seats: 4–6

Considering all the aircraft has to offer, the Seneca seems to be a good deal on the airplane market right now. Current prices vary from the low $40,000 range all the way up to $135,000, with most around $80,000. Shown is a Seneca II.

more than turning the prop around to make an engine run backwards. Even the starter has to spin in an opposite direction.

In 1975, Piper introduced the Seneca II, changing the engines to turbocharged Continental TSIO-360s in the process. The horsepower stayed the same at 200, but the airplane now could operate above 20,000ft. Rate of climb from sea level stayed at 1,340fpm, but the turbo could outclimb the standard Seneca above 7,000ft. Useful load on the turbo climbed 182lb over the normally-aspirated airplane's 1,600lb, but a lot of it got eaten up with options and avionics. Seating for all models stayed at six to seven, the seventh seat optional. You have to watch the weight and balance when loading all seven seats as it's possible to go outside the envelope with all the seats filled and too much fuel.

Just like the Cherokee Six, the Seneca has a cavernous door on the left side of the airplane, capable of swallowing objects up to 4ft wide by 2ft high. Plenty of room to stuff in that odd statue that Aunt Martha picked up during the last trip to Cancun. The Seneca has a station-wagon-like 13ft by 4ft by 4ft cabin capable of swallowing more cargo than any other plane in its class.

In 1975, Piper updated the Seneca to the Series II by adding turbocharged Continental TSIO-360 engines, rated at 200hp at sea level—215hp at 12,000ft. Also, they bumped up the useful load from the original 1,550lb to

This cutaway of a 1974 Seneca shows the general layout of the airplane and the cabin, with seating for six.

1,720lb. This gave the airplane the capability to load four people and luggage for an 800nm trip, with 45min reserves at the end of the flight. When all six seats are filled, the range comes down somewhat, depending on how much fuel must be traded for cabin load, but, even with the fuel-passenger tradeoff, the Seneca II's range is greater than any of its competitors' ranges. The Seneca II was discontinued in 1988.

While the Seneca will accommodate a large useful load, Piper was playing it safe when these shots were made; those are boxes of flowers going aboard and our hero is probably not too worried about over-grossing the aircraft with this cargo.

Another view of the Seneca's cargo door arrangement. This really is a practical arrangement if you've got a lot of bulky or awkward parcels (or, for that matter, people) to haul around.

The Seneca's throttle quadrant was designed to be more readily accessible than on some of the earlier models.

My CPA owns a Seneca II that he uses to fly from San Jose to his vacation home at Palm Springs. He packs three people plus himself, loads of baggage and food for the duration into the Seneca. He says it's still got more room for another set of golf clubs or a dog or two. He actually packs his dirty laun-

An affinity for the game of golf seems to be an important qualification for owning a Piper twin; the factory shots always seem to show Mr. Proud Pilot stashing a set of clubs into the cargo compartment.

dry back home on the return flight. Says that it's easier to clean at home than in Palm Springs when he should be out on a golf course. He's the CPA and he owns the Seneca, while I own a Macintosh SE/30, so I think he knows of what he speaks.

Seneca 200T and 220T Specifications

Engines:
200T—Continental L/TSIO-360E, 200hp, 1,400hr TBO
220T—Continental L/TSIO-360-KB, 220hp, 1,800hr TBO
Maximum Weight:
200T—4,570lb
220T—4,773lb
Fuel Capacity:
200T—98gal (standard); 128gal (optional)
220T—93gal
Maximum Speed:
200T—193kt
220T—196kt
Cruise Speed:
200T—190kt
220T—193kt
Fuel Consumption:
200T—23.6gph
220T—29gph
Range:
200T—546nm
220T—462nm
Rate of Climb at Sea Level:
200T—1,340fpm
220T—1,400fpm
Service Ceiling: 25,000ft
Takeoff Ground Run:
200T—900ft
220T—920ft
Takeoff over 50ft Obstacle:
200T—1,240ft
220T—1,210ft
Landing Ground Roll:
200T—1,380ft
220T—1,400ft
Landing over 50ft Obstacle:
200T—2,090ft
220T—2,160ft
Stall Speed: (flaps extended)
200T—61kt
220T—62kt
Standard Empty Weight:
200T—2,857lb
220T—2,875lb
Maximum Useful Load:
200T—1,713lb
220T—1,898lb
Wing Span: 38.9ft
Length: 28.5ft
Height: 9.9ft
Seats: 4–6

Piper tucked switch panels almost anywhere they could find room in the Seneca's cockpit, including this one on the port side, by the pilot's left knee.

The trim wheel is stashed between the seats, on the deck in this tidy little console along with the fuel cutoff switches.

Full deice protection is available for FAA-certified flight into known icing conditions, making the Seneca II a year-round airplane. Water skiing or snow skiing, the Seneca II will get you there, usually above all the weather. Although, why someone would want to fly 3hr through snow and ice just to strap long appendages on their feet so that they can fall down and be cold is beyond me. Warm water and sunbathing for me, any day.

The available avionics packages show no surprises. All Senecas carry a full complement of radios and navigation equipment, be it King, Narco, or Collins. Piper continued the practice of offering avionics packages of different levels with factory-installed prices running from $11,105 to $16,860. The last panel I looked at, came with Collins radios, ADF, transponder, two VORs, Northstar loran, Piper autopilot with altitude hold, full copilot instrumentation, intercom, and full deice panel. Everything except a stormscope or radar, the two options I'd add if I planned on lots of hard IFR.

The Seneca III appeared in 1989. It had the same Continental TSIO-360 turbocharged engines, now rated at 220hp on the same basic airframe. The Seneca II was discontinued in 1991. Piper says that the actual year model of the airplane is determined by the date of the original airworthiness certificate; therefore, check aircraft records to determine year.

The first Senecas are currently bringing $35,000 for a high-time 1972 to $59,000 for a

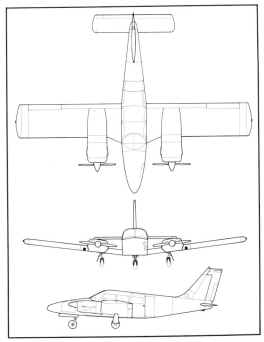

A three-view drawing of the PA-34 Seneca.

good, low TT model of the same year. A 1981 Seneca II with everything except a coke machine, is being offered at $129,000, about what the base aircraft, without avionics, cost new. The newest Seneca III on the market, a 1991, had an asking price of exactly what the owner paid for it in 1991, $383,500.

Any Seneca is a good investment. Along with being an excellent airplane for someone wanting to move up to an all-weather, 200mph twin, the Seneca, properly maintained, will return all your purchase price when it comes time to move up to that Cheyenne 400 LS.

Navajo

Back in 1974, a PA-31 Turbo Navajo B could be had for $129,990, without avionics. In 1993, a 180hp Piper Archer, listed at $163,000, is being given away by Sporty's Pilot Shop just for ordering anything from their shop. (If you want to try, the contest ends July 1994.) A lot has changed in 20 years.

Navajo Rating
Investment: #4
Utility: #2
Popularity: #2

The PA-31 Navajo tribe lived long and prospered. The aircraft was offered from 1967 until 1982 in many variants and sub-models. This is one of the very first, advertised as a six- to nine-place twin intended for corporate, private, and commuter airline service. It was offered from the start with and without turbo. Several cabin arrangements were offered, including one with a lavatory.

The cabin-class Navajo was introduced as Piper's entry into the business-class-twin market. Most of the airplanes are used for hauling four to six people over a 500nm trip, although a few work with feeder airlines or small commuter businesses. Some spend their time hauling canceled checks or small packages with a delivery service.

The Navajo has appeared in several variations. The initial-year airplane, 1967, was a non-pressurized, retractable twin equipped with two 310hp Lycoming turbocharged engines. It would cruise at high altitude for 900 miles with six people on board at 215kt. As time progressed, the Navajo became a 425hp pressurized airplane in 1970, gained 325hp C/R engines in 1975, and was discontinued in 1983.

Turbocharging helped the engines maintain their full 310hp rating up to 15,000ft. Single-engine flight can be sustained at the same altitude, but its rate of climb above 10,000ft is less than 200fpm. If you lose an engine and have high terrain ahead of you, your home airport behind you, and the throttle on the remaining engine all the way to the bulkhead, better that you plan a 180 back home rather than try to continue on. The higher powered Navajos, with 325hp, counter-rotating engines, are better able to handle engine-out

---

Navajo Typical Specifications
Engines: Lycoming TIO-540-A2C, 310hp, 1,800hr TBO
Maximum Weight: 6,536lb
Fuel Capacity: 187.3gal
Maximum Speed: 227kt
Cruise Speed: 215kt at 75% power at 22,000ft
Range: 995nm at 12,000ft; 1,005nm at 20,000ft
Rate of Climb at Sea Level: 1,445fpm
Single Engine Rate of Climb: 245fpm
Service Ceiling: 26,300ft
Single Engine Service Ceiling: 15,200ft
Takeoff Ground Run: 1,030ft
Takeoff over 50ft Obstacle: 2,190ft
Landing Ground Roll: 906ft
Landing over 50ft Obstacle: 1,818ft
Stall Speed: 70kt
Standard Empty Weight: 4,003lb
Maximum Useful Load: 2,533lb
Wing Span: 40.7ft
Length: 32.6ft
Height: 13ft
Seats: 6–8

The Navajo C/R. The "C/R" means "counter-rotating" props. This version was offered from 1975 to 1983. Published cruise speed is 220kt at 20,000ft, range is 940nm, rate of climb is 1,500fpm, and it could zoom right up to 26,400ft.

conditions than their smaller relative, so if you plan a lot of over-mountain or generally high terrain flying, look for one of the C/Rs, built starting in 1975.

The biggest reason for counter-rotation, however, is the inherent stability gained by having the engines turn in opposite directions. The three-bladed props provide balanced power for directional control in all situations. Should either engine quit, the resultant rudder correction required for stable flight is minimized.

The Navajo comes with an airstair door. It splits horizontally to give a three-step ramp for boarding the airplane—you don't climb into a Navajo, you walk aboard it just like on

Even the Navajo B served as a short-haul commuter airplane. Here's one disgorging a passel of passengers at Dulles International.

The PA-31 Navajo isn't a light twin trainer, but a working airplane that will haul over a ton halfway across the country on a single bound. This is the B version, identifiable by the four side windows. The C got five and the Chieftain has six.

The Navajos have engine-nacelle baggage compartments that allow long items, such as skis, to be stowed conveniently.

the big airplanes. If all eight seats are filled, the luggage compartment in the nose can be loaded with 150lb, and the aft space can bring the total up to 350lb. Just be sure to watch the weight and balance when loading the nose. It's possible to end up with the center of gravity too far forward under certain conditions.

Pilots and copilots have a flight deck that is not only professional, but also has enough comfort to make a 10hr day flying commuters fairly pleasant. Both seats up front are adjustable fore, aft, vertical, and for recline. Not too many pilots will be using the reclining

feature on a 300-mile trip, I would imagine. It might be a way to relax while waiting for the last cargo of canceled checks to arrive, though.

As with Piper's standard practice, the avionics for the Navajo are set up as a package deal. In 1979, five different packages were available, starting at $28,545 for the basic IFR package and climbing to $68,615 for a 150lb load of avionics from King and Collins. This pretty much included everything except a blender to make drinks for the passengers. There was a long list of options for those who wanted to uprate some of the existing radios

No golf clubs this time, just regular luggage for the Navajo's nose baggage compartment.

The aircraft may be smaller on the outside than many modern commuter aircraft, but the seating seems a lot roomier.

and autopilots in the standard packages. A Bendix GCS-810 autopilot/flight director (FD) could replace the standard two-axis King autopilot for another $5,235. This included an HSI slaved in with the autopilot and VOR/Loc/GS/longitudinal electric trim and a V-bar director horizon. What this means to those like me, still in the "manual trim and hold the yoke" stage, is that all the flight information is presented on one instrument, the HSI, and Bendix's autopilot will fly the airplane for you, right down to final approach on an instrument flight.

There is some truth to the adage that, "The bigger they get, the easier they are to fly." Although, a pilot uprating into the Navajo, after spending 250hr dragging an Apache through the air, might find argument with that; the truth is, the actual flying of the airplane gets easier as the size increases. Back in 1986, I had the rare pleasure to fly in a Grumman HU-16 Albatross from Reno, Nevada, to Oshkosh, Wisconsin, for the annual Experimental Aircraft Association (EAA) fly-in. The Albatross is a twin-engine amphibian that was used by the Navy as a search and rescue airplane. This one had been recovered from the boneyard at Davis-Monthan AFB, near Tucson, Arizona, and fully restored by the man who was crew chief on that very airplane when it was stationed at Guantanamo (GITMO), Cuba.

```
Navajo PA-31-325 Specifications
Engines: Lycoming TIO-540-F2BD and LTIO-540-F2BD,
    325hp, 1,800hr TBO
Maximum Weight: 6,540lb
Fuel Capacity: 183.5gal
Cruise at 75% Power: 220kt at 20,000ft
Cruise at 55% power: 180kt at 16,000ft
Range at 75% Power: 940nm at 20,000ft
Range at 55% Power: 1,040nm at 16,000ft
Rate of Climb at Sea Level: 1,500fpm
Single Engine Rate of Climb: 255fpm
Service Ceiling: 26,400ft
Single Engine Service Ceiling: 15,300ft
Takeoff Ground Run: 990ft
Takeoff over 50ft Obstacle: 2,080ft
Landing Ground Roll: 906ft
Landing over 50ft Obstacle: 1,818ft
Stall Speed: 70kt (flaps extended)
Standard Empty Weight: 4,099lb
Maximum Useful Load: 2,441lb
Wing Span: 40.7ft
Length: 32.6ft
Height: 13ft
Seats: 6–8
```

The trip was one of the high points of my life. The owner of the Albatross had brought along a 747 pilot who used to fly the old amphibian down in the South Pacific, way back when. While stopped for refueling in Scottsbluff, Nebraska, he commented that he had become spoiled driving 747s, and forgot how much more work the older planes required.

Here's a 1980 Navajo C/R climbing up out of the clouds en route to some distant destination, giving us a good look at its head on layout. It is a handsome machine overall, one of the prettiest reciprocating-engine twins.

This overhead shot shows the extended engine nacelles and general layout of the Navajo C/R. You can see the long, trailing portion of the engine nacelles in this shot—they also offer baggage stowage room.

Funny, when I got to spend 3hr in the left seat on the final hop, I didn't think that it was hard to fly at all. I also wasn't piloting a big Boeing for a living.

At the time, I owned a Harvard Mk. IV (Canadian AT-6 Texan) and it was a big step up to an airplane that weighed 16,000lb and whose main tanks had to be checked with a stick *after* $500 worth of $1.39-per-gallon avgas had been pumped in. I think the best part of the whole trip was when we landed at Oshkosh, reversed the props, and backed into the tie-down. Interesting sight.

Back to the Navajo and its flight systems. Color radar, a full set of copilot's instruments, radio altimeter, back-up power supply, and even an international package for global flights could be checked off the Approved Options Package when ordering a Navajo. Like a lot of other 10- to 20-year-old medium twins, the panel in most Navajos has probably been updated at least once. Most of them flying today have some sort of loran or GPS installed, plus a stormscope stacked alongside the color radar.

Some selling points to look for include: new deice boots, fresh paint (not a small matter as a paint job can easily run $10,000), larger 242gal fuel capacity, air conditioning, oxygen, winglets, props, and cargo door. Engine time plays a great part in determining value.

The book says $27,000 per side, but the book isn't doing the work. Count on $35,000 minimum for firewall forward and you won't be far off. The actual price of an engine rebuild depends a lot upon what you and your rebuilder work out, as every engine overhaul presents unique problems and must be handled on a one-on-one basis. The majority of piston engines need to be overhauled at 85 percent of TBO. Bluebook prices are based on mid-time engines using this percentage. Average overhaul costs are estimated average field costs, which don't include prop overhauls and other extras.

Average price for a 1980 Navajo, either C/R or standard, with 5,300hr TT and engines at 1,400hr, is $119,000, give or take $4,000. Go back a few years to 1968 and the same airplane can be had for $75,000 with 1,300 fewer hours on the airframe. Partially due to the increased cost of pressurization, the 1977 P-Navajo retails for 10 percent less than the Navajo C/R. About $116,000 will buy a nice, low engine time, air conditioned P-Navajo, ready to go to work flying commuters. Most Blue Book prices represent 40 percent of new price and dropping, so a Navajo isn't going to make any money for you on appreciation. Remember to bring someone who knows what it should look like, not what it does look like.

Chieftain

Take a Navajo, any Navajo, and stretch the fuselage from 32.6ft to 34.6ft, plug in 350hp turbocharged Lycoming engines, bump the gross weight to 7,000lb and, presto, you have a PA-31 Chieftain. The airframe's similar to the non-pressurized Navajo C/R, with one more window the only visual difference. The unpressurized cabin can be configured as two-seat cargo, eight-seat corporate, four-seat executive, or executive with a hot/cold refreshment center including a comfort unit replete with toilet and storage provisions behind an aft cabin folding door. The Chieftain was built from 1973 to 1984.

The Chieftain's multiple utility makes it a logical choice for a wide variety of owners—corporations, commuter and charter, government and military operations. The Chieftain fits in above the Navajo and the pressurized Navajo completing the lineup derived from

The Navajo Chieftain is a ten-place business air-craft. Its primary use is as a commuter aircraft feed-ing to a central jet hub. Many have also been used to ferry cargo such as canceled checks.

the same PA-31 airframe. The Chieftain's 1,090-mile range, covered in less than five hours, lets you flight plan for one long-hop cross-country, or a series of shorter flights, without the necessity of refueling.

A lot of the Chieftains spend their days as commuters, moving nine people and the pilot with US air carriers. Hundreds of them are busy shuttling people throughout the world.

Most of the trips are within 500 miles, taking advantage of the 221kt cruise to make short work of moving passengers from a satellite airport to an international hub for connection to jet service. Quite a load of luggage can be carried outside the cabin in wing lockers located in the aft portion of the engine nacelles or in the 200lb capacity nose compartment. Packing a ton of cargo instead of passengers,

The Chieftain is a stretched Navajo, accommodating up to ten folks in reasonable comfort. It's been successful in the short-haul airline business, and there are rather a lot of them around. That long proboscis accommodates baggage.

111

This angle shows off the three-bladed props and gear configuration. Chieftains are selling for about $130,000 (up to $300,000 plus for the nearly new ones) in the current market.

an IFR-equipped Chieftain with one pilot can carry fuel for 400 miles, still maintaining 45min reserves.

One neat feature about the series is that the interior can be reconfigured from passenger, to corporate, to hauling truck tires in the space of an hour. Air conditioning is available to cool the cabin prior to loading and provides dehumidified air throughout the flight when used as a people hauler. Cargo doesn't care if it's hot or cold, so some Chieftains will have been ordered without air conditioning.

With the double doors and cargo capacity, the Chieftain gets used for a kind of airborne UPS truck, taking priority packages—one of its principal uses. Note that the pilot's window opens to allow airflow during those long waits for a taxi clearance at some airports, and emergency egress when the cabin is full of boxes and smoke at the same time.

If you fly out of Phoenix and can't stand cabin temperatures just slightly under the melting point of lead, make sure the airplane you buy has refrigerated air. Adding air conditioning down the road gets to be a very expensive proposition. In 1979, air was a $6,000 option; today, it might be cost prohibitive to retrofit.

As far as panel and options, anything available on the Navajo can cross into the Chieftain. Fuel tanks can be built into the wing lockers to bring the total capacity to 242gal. Telephone, stereo, VCR, tinted windows, and leather upholstery add enough luxury for any owner. There's no real end to what can be fitted in the Chieftain as far as elegance and comfort: teak hand-crafted cabinetry, a vanity, lavatory convenience, hot and cold drinks—all the little things to take one's mind off the drudgery of flying.

A nice little point for the pilot is a window/door right next to his left elbow, that can be opened before flight. Handy if you want to check oil in the left engine before starting it.

Chieftain Rating
Investment: #3
Utility: #1
Popularity: #2

The Navajo Chieftain has tremendous load carrying capacity, and when stripped of extra seats and other non-essentials it can be converted to an excellent little cargo airplane. With the seats left in, it is a handy way for companies with far-flung projects to check up on progress—although this works best if those projects are about 500 miles apart because there is no avoiding the truth that the cabin is tighter than a commercial airliner's cabin. But it can get in and out of the many little airports around the country (and the world) that don't see scheduled airliners, including strips as short as 2,500–3,000ft.

As you will gather by now, all prices are driven by condition and time on the aircraft. Late-seventies models can be found with zero-time engines for $150,000. A 1984 model, the last year built, goes for $325,000; an older, more tired high-timer that spent all its life moving boxes from tedium to apathy, will sell in the $90,000 range. Here you really get what

Pressurized Navajos weren't produced in large numbers. There are, nonetheless, usually about a dozen to choose from in *Trade-A-Plane,* and the ones in the current issue are ranging from about $90,000 to $120,000, depending on engine time and radios. The great virtue of the airplane is that you can go up to FL 20 without a bag of oxygen on your face. The 31P looks pretty much like other members of the Navajo tribe, but there are only three windows on the side, the fuselage is a bit rounder, and the extended nacelles and their baggage stowage have been discarded.

you pay for—the ideal being to make sure you don't have to pay for it multiple times after you buy.

Mojave

Built for only one year, the PA-31 Mojave is a pressurized, turbocharged 350hp iteration of the trusty Navajo airframe. The smaller Navajo is primarily a business airplane, while the bigger Chieftain goes to work hauling cargo and/or commuters, but their marketing and missions were similar. The Mojave really didn't fit anywhere—hence only one year of production.

Somewhere around fifty serial numbers were assigned to the Mojave; whether they were all built is a good guess. The airplane is

quite similar to the Chieftain, only with a pressurized cabin. They are rather hard to locate ten years later; most trade papers don't show a separate listing for the model. Unless you absolutely have to have one, I'd recommend that you approach with caution any for sale. Not that they are a bad airplane; it's just that others will do the same job without the high expense of maintaining the pressure vessel on the Mojave.

As with other airplanes, some STCs were issued for the Mojave giving it more horsepower or higher gross weight. One swap is to the 425hp Lycoming TIGSO-541-E1A engines and a bump up in the gross weight from 7,245lb to 7,800lb, which makes the airplane more useful as a load hauler.

A good older Cheyenne II will give more performance with 620hp Pratt & Whitney turbines for about the same cost. Granted, it costs a lot more to overhaul a P&W turbine than a Lycoming TIO-540, but the P&W's TBO is 3,500hr, nearly twice as long as the Lycoming's 2,000hr TBO.

The Blue Book shows the 1984 Mojave's resale at $310,000. I was unable to find any for sale, so I guess we go with that. If I was looking, I'd try to work the price down to the $250,000 range, but that's up to you. Good luck!

Chapter 8

The Kerosene Indians

Cheyenne I and II

Piper's first entry into the turboprop market was introduced in 1974 as the PA-31T Cheyenne (later the Cheyenne II, when the Cheyenne I came on line in 1978). The Cheyenne was a Navajo airframe fitted with two Pratt & Whitney turbine engines producing 620shp. The Cheyenne II XL, introduced in 1981, has the fuselage stretched 2ft, but is otherwise similar to the Cheyenne II. Both airplanes were offered together until the market forced discontinuance in 1983. Some XLs are shown as 1984 models, but Piper goes by when the airworthiness certificate was issued to determine model year, so calendar year and certificate year may differ.

The PA-31 Cheyenne I is not, as you would expect, the first of the breed. The I is, instead, the stripped down, economy version; if it were a car it wouldn't have hubcaps or a radio. The Cheyenne I has less powerful engines and fewer features than the other models. It was introduced in 1978, nine years after the basic design first flew. It is shorter than the Cheyenne II by 2ft, and some Cheyenne I models don't even have tip tanks.

Cheyenne I and II Rating
Investment: #3
Utility: #2
Popularity: #3 (#4 with SAS)

Either model will cruise 275kt at altitude for over 1,000nm with a cabin full of people and baggage. Built to compete with other turboprops such as the Beach C-90 at E-90 King Air, the Cheyenne pulls out a 30kt lead over the more palatial Beech C-90, and holds its own against the King Air E-90 at 288kt.

The King Air has a larger cabin usually outfitted like a luxury hotel, with more room to wander about, but the pilot-owners of the Cheyenne seem to appreciate the lean-and-mean image of the Piper, and they are willing to put up with the smaller cabin on their way up to the left seat.

The Cheyenne II has been beset by a flying characteristic, since its inception, that has kept some buyers away, and held down the resale somewhat. The Cheyenne's 620shp turbines are 500lb lighter and far more powerful than the Lycoming 540ci engines they replaced. As a result, the Cheyenne was unstable in the pitch axis. Piper's solution to the lack of stability was to install a stability augmentation system (SAS) to add some push to the control yoke under certain conditions, mainly at high power and a CG back at the aft limit. This usually occurs during initial take-off rotation, and during climbout. The Cheyenne would go dead on the stick under these conditions. Not that the yoke wouldn't respond, just that it could be pulled back out of trim and stay there, as speed bled off, instead of returning to the previous trimmed airspeed. If the SAS was inoperative, the flight had to be scrubbed.

Piper lost two major lawsuits involving the Cheyenne and its SAS back in the mid-eighties. The suits were in response to two crashes and fourteen deaths. Some people said that the airplane, even with the SAS, was not stable, causing the accidents. They even went so far as to say the SAS could cause the airplane to go into wild pitch oscillations when a nose-down situation was initiated. Piper paid, but the National Transportation Safety Board (NTSB), after extensive investigation, announced that it found no unsafe conditions in the Cheyenne.

The principal cause of the crashes was determined by the NTSB to be lack of training

Here's Piper's first turbine-powered model, first flown in 1969. The Cheyenne II has seating for eight, and was built in three variations, the Cheyenne I with less power, the II with PT6A engines, and the IIXL, a stretched version. The Cheyenne II will plug along at about a 244mph cruise.

for the pilots and, in one situation, an airplane loaded past its aft CG limits. This further reinforces the idea that you just can't step out of a Seminole, get a day or two of training, and go fly a high-performance turbine twin. People like Flight Safety International (1-800-227-5656) provide excellent classroom and simulator training to help maintain proficiency in the Cheyenne, or any other big Piper.

In 1978 the Cheyenne I was introduced. The aft CG position was moved forward 2in, and the engines were downsized to 500shp. This cut 1,000fpm off the initial climb rate and chopped the cruise speed by 40kt. Like going from the Corvette ZR-1 to the LT-1, you lose a little power, the price goes down. Also, the dreaded SAS was not required on the Cheyenne I. So what you got was a slower airplane without augmentation that should be safer to fly.

The Cheyenne II XL appeared in 1981 and disappeared in 1984, fewer than 80 having been built. It has a 2ft stretch ahead of the main spar, P&W PT6A-135 turbines—rated 620shp per side and no SAS. The II XL's eight seats can be filled, 400lb of luggage can be loaded fore and aft, and the tanks can be almost filled while keeping within the CG limits. This would give you 4.5hr in the air, covering over 1,100nm with full reserves. All this and 250kt, too.

The Cheyenne IA debuted in 1984 and 12 months later it was gone from the inventory. In its one-year life span, approximately 20 planes sold. The main changes from the Cheyenne I were standard wing tanks and redesigned engine nacelles. For this you get about 12kt more up high and a market price in 1993 of $660,000.

If you are an individual pilot who wants to own a high performance, relatively low maintenance 250kt airplane and are willing to keep up with the training, then an early Cheyenne should be high on the list of what you want to see in your hangar.

As far as an average price on a Cheyenne I or II, the market runs from $310,000 for a 1974 Cheyenne to $805,000 for a late production Cheyenne IA. Your bank account will be the limiting force as far as which one will be yours.

Cheyenne III, IIIA, and 400 LS

In 1979, a new look appeared at Piper. The new airplane, PA-42 Cheyenne III, sported a T-tail 17ft off the ground. Overall, it was a bigger airplane than its predecessors, having greater wing span, longer fuselage, more windows, and uprated engines to go along with the prominent tail. One 680shp engine per side powered the III up to 33,000ft, where it boomed along at 300kt cruise, packing eight

Cheyenne III, IIIA, and 400 LS Rating
Investment: #2
Utility: #2
Popularity: #4

The PA-42 Cheyenne III is a T-tailed business twin and a fast, fancy turboprop that went on the market back in 1980. Two years later, the Cheyenne III made a globe-hopping trip in just 88 flying hours. Depending on how the cabin is set up, between six and eleven passengers can be transported. Tip tanks were optional. The Cheyenne III is rated at a 318mph cruise.

passengers in corporate seating or four when fitted out as an executive mover.

The Cheyenne IIIA went into production in January 1984 with two more powerful engines and some slight changes to the interior. The Cheyenne III will bring around $770,000 today, holding less than half of its new-equipped price of $1,621,094. The IIIA, with

---

Cheyenne III and IIIA Typical Specifications
Engines: Pratt & Whitney PT6A-61, 720shp, 3,000hr TBO
Maximum Weight: 11,285lb
Maximum Speed: 301kt
Cruise Speed: 301kt at 75% power
Range: 2,270nm
Rate of Climb: 2,380fpm
Service Ceiling: 38,840ft
Single Engine Service Ceiling: 17,100ft
Takeoff over 50ft Obstacle: 2,280ft
Landing over 50ft Obstacle: 3,043ft
Maximum Useful Load: 4,448lb
Seats: 9–11
Wing Span: 47.7ft
Length: 43.4ft
Height: 17ft

low-cycle turbines, will market in the $1.2 million range, few being available for me to test fly at this date.

Here is where the one logbook for the airframe and the two for the turbines become very important. Look for a Cheyenne that's been maintained by one of the Piper distributors. Make sure that all the paperwork authenticates the entries in the logbook. If you own the airplane for 10 years, or better, the initial cost of the airplane will be equaled by the amount spent to operate and maintain it—make sure it's right from the start.

Let's say I just won the California Lottery; hit it big for thirty mil. What would I treat myself to in an airplane? Well, in Piper's case it would have to be the Cheyenne 400 LS introduced in 1984. With 1,000shp per side for motivation, a go-fast speed of 358kt for 1,800 miles with me and my significant other on board, I'd be gone in 60sec. This airplane and an unlimited Gold Card would make for a very nice way to see the countryside.

The 400 LS can get into unimproved runways that would make a Seneca nervous, to say nothing of most of the business jets. It will carry sea-level atmosphere to 18,500ft, climbing to a cabin altitude of 9,980ft at 41,000ft. Built as Piper's flagship from 1984 to 1991, like so many others, it's no longer in production. Not a whole lot of them were sold over their eight-year life span, probably due to the pressure from entry-level bizjets. A fully equipped 1987 400 LS sold new for $2.8 million, right around the same price as a Cessna Citation 550 SP—a 390kt jet cruiser. People wanted the panache of not having propellers on their airplane, so they went with the jet.

Judging by the serial numbers in the *Aircraft Bluebook,* as of 1991 not more than fifty had been made, so they are a bit rare. If Piper weathers the ongoing storms of ownership

Cheyenne 400 LS Specifications	
Engines:	Garrett TPE 331-14, 1,000shp, 3,000hr TBO
Maximum Weight:	12,135lb
Fuel Capacity:	570gal usable
Cruise Speed:	358kt at 24,000ft; 347kt at 35,000ft
Range:	1,169–2,176nm
Rate of Climb:	3,242fpm
Service Ceiling:	41,000ft
Takeoff over 50ft Obstacle:	2,685ft
Landing over 50ft Obstacle:	2,805ft
Standard Empty Weight:	7,478lb
Maximum Useful Load:	4,589lb
Wing Span:	47.7ft
Length:	43.4ft
Height:	17ft
Seats:	9

changes and bankruptcy courts, it might return the 400 to production, but with the advent of Cessna's new CitationJet, Piper would be fighting stiff competition.

A 400 LS can be found for close to $1 million, but it will need work. Most models in the late eighties are selling for around $1.3–$1.6 million. I'd go seek out a broker who specializes in turboprops and has sold a few in his time. He would have more turboprops on hand, giving you a chance to get a feel for different airplanes.

T-1040 Commuter (1981)

Mentioned only briefly, the T-1040 was built in 1981 as a nine-passenger commuter airplane. Assembled out of the wings, nose and tail of the early Cheyenne, with the fuselage from the Chieftain, it is powered by two 500hp P&W turboprops. The idea didn't go far and only a few were built. They are very rare, so I have no idea as to what one would be worth.

Chapter 9

The Aerostar

Initially built in 1967 by aircraft genius Ted Smith, the Aerostar was sold to Piper in time for its appearance as a 1969. Touted as the fastest piston powered airplane, the pressurized 700P would easily cruise in the 265kt

The reason the PA-60 Aerostar doesn't look like a Piper is that it isn't a Piper. This piston-powered twin was originally called the Aerostar 600 (or the 601P, a pressurized version with a bit more wing span). It's been a fairly popular model, with about a thousand sold. The design is a bit unusual in that the wing is straight while the tail is swept; it is very unusual in that the fin and horizontal stabilizer surfaces are interchangeable. It was originally the product of a visionary named Ted Smith who tried to compete with the big boys with his elegant, mid-wing design. It was first flown in 1967 and became part of the Piper line in the late seventies. A more powerful version is known as the 700P. A 1980 Aerostar A is shown.

range. The 601P has 290hp per side, good for a 235kt cruise over 1,100nm. Even the normally-aspirated 600 can cruise at 218kt. Any model you choose, you get speed. Ted Smith built the airplane as a personal transport to cover a lot of ground in a hurry. He believed that the primary reason for owning an airplane was to go somewhere fast. He incorporated all the go-fast secrets he knew in the first Aerostar.

Piper took the design and refined it into the airplane we see today. It's slick, it's fast, and it's real tight around the shoulders. Like Mooney with their fast singles, Aerostar gets a lot of its swoosh by being small.

Boarding the airplane is a bit unusual. There is only one airstair door to enter the airplane, next to the pilot. The pilot's seat has to move forward before anyone can reach the aft seats. The pilot's the last aboard. If, for some reason, the person in the last rear seat wants to get up and leave before the door is shut, the pilot has to deplane and move his seat forward to allow the person to get out.

It a very pretty airplane from any angle. If looks drive you, and a lot of speed won't hurt, go check out an Aerostar. Try to find

---

Aerostar Rating
Investment: #2
Utility: #3 (It's a toy with wings)
Popularity: #1 (It's a toy with wings)

You could buy an Aerostar 600A just like this for only $79,000, complete with radar, loran, a pair of King 170Bs with glideslope, de-icing, and all sorts of neat stuff; total time on the beast—only about 4,800hr, with about 1,200hr on the left engine and about 1,500hr on the right. Another one with fresher engines is going for about double that.

one that has had the Machen 700 conversion to 350hp engines, along with other modifications such as intercoolers and different props.

Most of the Aerostars I've had the pleasure to become acquainted with have been

Here's a 1981 B model, motoring along in Aerostar splendor. The aircraft is popular enough to have its own fan club, the Aerostar Owners Association; they can be reached at (912) 244-7827. Their mag-azine provides the hot scoop on FAA alerts and cautions, as well as the usual enthusiast information.

treated by their owners as one of the family. It's very possible to locate a hangared 1982 Aerostar with less than 1,600hr TT on the airframe, and 150hr on both engines. Usually it will have all sorts of navigation equipment in the panel—radar, stormscope, radar altimeter, loran, GPS, just to name a few. I recently ran across a 1977 601B, total time 1,170hr, all by the same owner. It has full Collins radios along with many other modifications; it lived in a hangar all its life with its one owner. Were I looking—I'd be calling.

In 1988, two of us took a Beech Debonair (225hp) all the way down the west coast of Mexico for a ten-day vacation. We eventually ended up in Puerto Escondido, a small fishing village rapidly on its way to becoming a resort. It's 164nm below Acapulco, so it doesn't see many American tourists in light airplanes. We were the first arrivals that week. We even had a welcoming committee composed of the airport manager and tower operator. (Tower operator—yes, things were that slow.) As we got ready to depart for home (after too many Margaritas, too much shrimp, and too much sun), we met a couple flying their Aerostar 601 coming back from San Pedro Sula, in Honduras.

They had been down checking out the ruins at Copan for a week and were on their way back to Tucson for the same reasons as we were. We got into a friendly discussion about how my airplane was slower than a hand-pushed taco wagon, and the 601 owner graciously offering to let my girlfriend ride with him in a *fast* airplane. She was kind enough to refuse the ride, knowing that it is a long walk from Tucson to our home in San Jose. We ended up taking a bet as to how much faster his airplane would cover the 1,600nm trip to home. We agreed to stop in Guaymas, on the coast near Hermosillo, for the night.

Well, even with the long-range tanks in the Debonair, they were showered, napped, and on their second drink by the time we came trudging into the Playa de Cortez Hotel. That's when I decided my next airplane would have two engines and enough power to pull the skin off a chocolate pudding. That turned out to be a Cessna O-2A, and that's *definitely* a story for another book.

The point being, if you want a twin-engine rocket ship for personal transportation, go find an Aerostar. If you don't want the added maintenance of pressurization, find a

The Aerostar 601Ps seem to be especially common and available with prices running in the vicinity of $150,00 for examples tricked out with the normal bells and whistles.

600, 601, or 601B. They all have the Lycoming engines, good for 2,000hr between rebuilds, and most of them make it to TBO without major problems. You should be able to find a nice, low-time one for around $90,000. Treat it right and it will bring back all that money when it's time to sell.

Aerostar 600 and 700P Typical Specifications

Engines:
600—Lycoming IO-540, 290hp, 2,000hr TBO
700P—Lycoming TIO-540, 350hp, 1,800hr TBO

Maximum Weight:
600—6,029lb
700P—6,315lb

Maximum Speed:
600—226kt
700P—257kt

Cruise:
600—220kt
700P—230kt

Range:
600—1,150nm
700P—1,160nm

Rate of Climb:
600—2,400fpm
700P—1,840fpm

Service Ceiling:
600—25,000ft
700P—25,000ft

Stall Speed: 71kt

Takeoff over 50ft Obstacle:
600—2,194ft
700P—3,080ft

Landing over 50ft Obstacle:
600—1,500ft
700P—2,140ft

Maximum Useful Load:
600—1,954lb
700P—2,081lb

Seats: 6

The Aerostar is a fast airplane, willing to cruise along at 280kt, and can slow down enough to drop in on short fields. It needs about 2,000ft to land, which opens up a lot of little airports around the country. When it is time to go, it will go upstairs almost as fast as a DC-9, up to 3,800fpm. And the only time it belongs down this low is on short final or when it's time to have its picture made.

Chapter 10

The Agricultural Indians

Piper was the first aircraft manufacturer to build an airplane strictly for the bug-killing business. The first agricultural plane off Piper's line was the 150hp PA-25 Pawnee in 1960. It didn't take Piper too long to figure out that 150hp just wasn't going to lift enough chemicals to make itself profitable. They powered the Pawnee with a 235hp engine in 1962, staying with it until the 260hp engine was added in 1969. Both versions of the sprayer continued to be built up to 1981 when the company was within one year of getting out of the ag-plane business. The last ag plane manufactured by Piper was the PA-36 Pawnee Brave 400, carrying the same monster-motor found in the Comanche 400.

All the ag planes have a relatively low TBO compared to the rest of the fleet. The Continental Tiara-6-285 has to be torn down every 1,200hr. The Lycoming IO-540 has a 1,500hr TBO. If you think about how these engines are operated, you can easily see why they would have to be rebuilt sooner than the general aviation engine of the same type. Getting up before it's light; having to run on auto fuel all day; working with the throttle hammered into the firewall, 50ft above the ground at 75mph dodging wires—no wonder an engine wears out fast. Most ag engines average 1,000hr TBO when run on mogas: there is a higher engine reserve for the 235 than the 260 because of the more frequent teardowns encountered.

The owners even hang bright lights under the airplane so that it can work all night when the bugs aren't flying and are easier to spray. Also, after the sun goes down, the air is much stiller—no wind makes for more even applications. From watching a Pawnee spray a field, I can see how the low wing helps disperse the load through downwash and swirl, aiding in penetration. The cockpit's far enough behind the wing for good visibility and pilot protection. I'm told by ag pilots that it's nice to have a lot of airplane in front of you if you hit something that won't move right away, like wires or poles.

A good ag plane can cover 6–7 acres per minute with either solids or liquids. When crops are too high to permit tractors to operate, the Pawnee can cover the area without compacting the soil or knocking down the crops.

When dealing with an ag plane, ease of maintenance is paramount. The Brave series can be disassembled—wings removed, fuselage stripped to bare frame, canopy and hopper readily removed. The frame of the Brave is steel truss, heli-arc welded chrome-moly tubing, rated for high energy absorption. The stuff that gets knocked off with heavy use, wing tips and belly panels, are removable and

> **Pawnee and Pawnee Brave Rating**
> Investment: #1
> Utility: #1 (What else can they do?)
> Popularity: #2 (The bugs hate 'em)

Before the Piper Pawnee came down the trail, ag planes were bastardized warbirds, trainers, utility, or light passenger airplanes. The Pawnee was designed from the ground up to be a crop duster, pure and simple. As a result it is a sturdy, slow, survivable airplane that isn't much good for anything except making money down in the weeds. The design was the result of advice from Cornell University studies that suggested the high cockpit, for improved visibility, and the long nose for improved crashworthiness. The Pawnee Brave is shown.

easily repairable. The side and belly panels can be popped off with quick-release fasteners in minutes for access to every fuselage component. The cockpit floor is sealed to keep

The pump for the sprayer system is driven by airflow. This detail shows the underside of the Pawnee Brave, complete with stiff steel gear and sprayer bar assembly.

all chemicals and bugs outside where they belong.

All the air entering the cockpit is run through a filter and force inducted for a positively pressurized cockpit. This ensures that all air flows from inside the cockpit high pressure area, to the lower pressure around the plane, keeping out the dust and chemicals.

As you might expect, there aren't a lot of avionics options offered for any of the ag planes. If you get a radio and transponder in the panel, consider that as close to IFR as your going to get. Not too many dusters work well in solid instrument meteorological conditions.

The D version of the Pawnee is shown scooting along in uncontrolled airspace at its working airspeed of 95mph. The Pawnee (the non-Brave version) can be identified from the Pawnee Brave most easily by noting that the Brave lacks wing or tail braces. The Pawnee was originally developed in 1972 and production was taken over by WTA, the Texas company that also continued production of the Cub after Piper dropped the models from their line-up.

Here's a cutaway of the 1978 Pawnee Brave 300 model. Most of the entire airplane is an access panel of one sort or another, and the rest is a strut or brace.

Not that they wouldn't try, if the pay was right.

Once you've hoisted yourself into the cockpit, you'll be surprised at the Spartan conditions you encounter. Sit down in the seat, move the shoulder harness so that the buckle doesn't rearrange important body parts, and sit down in a puff of dust. No, it's not the cleanest airplane you have sat in—probably leave a ring around your Levis. Look out between the post in the center of the windshield. If the plexiglass has been cleaned lately, you might just be able to see the ground on a 45-degree angle in front of you. The long nose precludes seeing directly in front of you.

Oh, the wire running from the windshield post to the rudder? No, it's not a radio antenna, it's a wire deflector. That's what keeps the cockpit (and the upper half of the pilot) from leaving the airplane, should it inadvertently meet up with a utility wire. Those strange chunks of metal on the main gear are wire cutters, in case you happen to be almost high enough to clear, but still catch a cable with the mains. As far as bigger obstacles, you're on your own. Just don't bend the airplane to where the guys can't repair it by tomorrow.

The Brave's maximum takeoff weight in the normal category (which nobody uses) is 3,900lb. In the restricted category, another 900lb can be lifted, but the landing weight stays the same, no matter what the takeoff load turns out to be. Maximum landing weight is 3,900lb. If something up front goes

---

Pawnee 235 and 260 Typical Specifications
Engine:
Lycoming O-540-B2B5, 235hp, 1,200hr TBO
Lycoming O-540-G1A5, 260hp, 1,500hr TBO
Maximum Weight: 2,900lb
Fuel Capacity: 38.5gal (36gal usable)
Maximum Speed: 124mph
Cruise Speed: 114mph
Fuel Consumption: 14gph
Range: 290nm
Rate of Climb: 700fpm
Takeoff Ground Run: 785ft
Takeoff Over 50ft Obstacle: 1,350ft
Landing Ground Roll: 850ft
Stall Speed with Flaps: 46mph
Standard Empty Weight: 1,420lb
Maximum Useful Load: 1,480lb
Hopper Load: 150gal of liquid or 1,200lb of solids
Wing Span: 36.2ft
Length: 24.7ft
Height: 7.2ft

Pawnee Brave 300 and 375
Typical Specifications
Engine:
300—Lycoming IO-540-K1G5, 300hp, 1,200hr TBO
375—Lycoming IO-720-D1CD, 375hp, 1,500hr TBO
Maximum Weight:
300—3,900lb
375—4,800lb
Fuel Capacity: 86gal
Maximum Speed:
300—148mph
375—160mph
Cruise Speed:
300—142mph
375—149mph
Range:
300—565 miles
375—605 miles
Rate of Climb at Sea Level:
300—770fpm
375—1,060fpm
Service Ceiling:
300—12,000ft
375—15,000ft
Takeoff over 50ft Obstacle:
300—1,525ft
375—1,150ft
Takeoff Ground Run:
300—960ft
375—700ft
Landing over 50ft Obstacle:
300—1,650ft
375—1,720ft
Landing Ground Roll:
300—700ft
375—770ft
Stall Speed with Flaps:
300—62mph
375—65mph
Standard Empty Weight:
300—2,180lb
375—2,434lb
Maximum Useful Load without Dispersal Equipment:
300—2,220lb
375—2,370lb.
Hopper Size: 225gal or 275gal of liquid, or 1,900lb of solids
Wing Span: 38.8ft
Length:
300—26.8ft
375—27.5ft
Height: 7.5ft

The wing braces on the Pawnee add a tremendous amount of stiffness—and drag. These airplanes seem to be selling for about $30,000 in the current market. All will have spent tremendous amounts of time aloft, twisting and turning, and nearly all will have been re-engined at least once by now.

Johnston Aircraft Service in Tulare, California, specializes in maintenance and modification of the Piper ag tribe, where this one was resting momentarily before heading back out to the local cotton fields. Johnston is the creator of the 400hp Super Brave.

blooey, causing the fan to quit, there's a quick dump feature on the hopper to keep you from arriving at the ground with a loud noise. Remember, you can be replaced, but it's got to fly tomorrow.

The specs show that at 75 percent power, a 375hp Brave can cruise at 149mph. I seriously think that few pilots have spent much time flying cross-country in a duster. Maybe jumping from one short strip to another, three counties away, but not load Mom and the kids in the hopper while Dad flies to Pine Ridge.

Later in its life, the Brave 375 got a shot of steroids in the motor department. In 1983, the same Lycoming 400hp engine that powers the Comanche 400 to 215mph was stuffed under the cowl. Twenty-five horses increase doesn't sound like a lot, nevertheless the difference in the takeoff run and load capacity is well worth the expense of the bigger engine. It's as close as Piper ever got to a gas turbine in a duster, and the biggest piston engine ever hung in a modern duster.

Both Cessna and Piper left the duster business in the same year, 1983. The competition from helicopters and larger turbine-powered ag planes took a lot of business away

from the two manufacturers. So, if you are in the ag-plane market, and want a Piper, remember, all these airplanes have worked for a living, and you can't make any money with the airplane tied down.

Say you want to run a sailplane business, and need a tow plane? Knowing how well they work as tugs, what could you find in the way of an older ag plane?

A 1963 Pawnee D-235, with 4,140hr TT, 60hr SMOH, said to be very clean, is priced at $27,500. A 400 Super Brave, 175hr on the engine, zero-timed prop, and high-lift wing kit, can go to work for you as soon as you part with $70,000. If you just want a Pawnee to help your glider business stay up, a 1966 without equipment, but with tow hook, can come home with you for $21,000. With these airplanes, more than any other, condition and damage history drive the price. As before, take someone who has spent many late nights working on one when you go to buy.

Look at the logbooks very carefully in comparison to the existing bills, receipts, and general aircraft condition. Remove some panels. If you find a good Lycoming-powered bug-blaster, the odds are excellent that you might make a little money when resale time rolls around.

Index